# Analog: A Play In Two Acts

Darryl Pickett

Published by Odsmil Press, 2023.

ANALOG: A PLAY IN TWO ACTS

**First edition. March 17, 2023.**

Copyright © 2023 Darryl Pickett.

ISBN: 979-8215819715

Written by Darryl Pickett.

# Table of Contents

For Stephanie Lauren Bramson

In Loving Memory

# Notice:

# Dramatis Personae

Analog was first presented at the Moonlight Players Warehouse Theater in Clermont, Florida from Oct. 27 - Nov. 2. The production was directed by Darryl Pickett. The cast, in order of appearance, was as follows:

**Simon Lexner** - *22, university student* - Michael Cleary

**Heather Grenado** - *20, fellow student* - Casey Dey

**Max Meier** - *64, record store owner* - Darryl Pickett

**Katarina** - *36, daughter of Johann* - Kim Luffman

**Uli Falkenrath** - *42, fiancé of Katarina* - Juan Santos

**Johann** - 59, musician - Marty Wicks

# Act One

Note: The play is performed in two uninterrupted acts. These have been broken down into separate scenes in this publication for rehearsal use, but scene titles need not be listed in programs or announced to the audience.

*Place: A Shop in Leipzig*

*Time: An Afternoon in September 2014*

*A large, antique wooden cabinet with several drawers and a wardrobe style door stands at the back of the stage. On it hangs a sign:*

Dr. Max

Musik und Antiquität *Music & Antiques*

Öffnen 0800 - 1800

*At stage right, there is a small table topped with one or two crates of vinyl records. Several more records, of eclectic origin, are placed around the shop.*

*Another small table is located stage left, on which sits a record turntable. Downstage of this is a digital piano, the back of which is draped. Set on the piano in a small frame is a watercolor painting of a butterfly. Two small chairs are placed near center stage, and a third nearby.*

# 1-A: The Shop

*At Lights Up, two young American students, SIMON LEXNER and HEATHER GRENADO, browse the shop. Simon wears a backpack. He is looking carefully through the record bin. Heather spots an album on open display and picks it up, showing it to Simon.*

**HEATHER** - Hey, I think I found it. Bach Partita Number Two. Right?

**SIMON** - Almost. Right piece, wrong artist. That's Johanna Martzy. She's fantastic. But she's not Irena Dobos.

**HEATHER** - Do you want to get it anyway?

**SIMON** - How much?

**HEATHER** - 75 Euros.

**SIMON** - Ouch. It'll have to wait.

**HEATHER** - Why are they so expensive?

**SIMON** - *(pointing at sticker on album cover)* "All-Analog. Mastered from the Original Tapes."

**HEATHER** - *(sarcastic)* Oooo ...

**SIMON** - Limited pressing of one thousand. Scarcity creates demand.

**HEATHER** - Sounds like a scam to me.

**SIMON** - You pay for quality. Believe me, there's a difference.

**HEATHER** - If you say so. Here's another Bach.

**SIMON** - *(takes the album from her and looks at it)* B Minor Mass. The Arcturus Ensemble. Never heard of them.

**HEATHER** - It's only 12. That's cheap, right?

**SIMON** - Very cheap. So probably not any good.

**HEATHER** - You don't know that. *(cell phone rings)* Hang on. *(answers)* David, where are you? ... Well, we found the record store. Simon is in heaven. It's all super expensive.

**SIMON** - Worth it!

**HEATHER** - Are you headed this way? ... I don't know. Hang on. *(To Simon)* How long do you think we're going to be here?

**SIMON** - I could stay all day.

**HEATHER** - David's hungry. He wants to grab an early dinner.

**SIMON** - That's fine.

**HEATHER** - That's fine, David. Just give us a call when you're done, okay? *(Ends call)*

**SIMON** - What's keeping him?

**HEATHER** - He wants to drop Composition and take Advanced Acoustics instead. They won't let him so he's arguing with admin.

**SIMON** - Is he arguing in English or *auf deutsch*?

**HEATHER** - His German is terrible. That's why it's taking so long.

**SIMON** - *(finding an album)* No way! Look. They have Irena! Bach Partitas for Solo Violin!

**HEATHER** - 400 Euros! You already have this on CD.

**SIMON** - Have I taught you nothing? This record was meant to be heard on vinyl! This is the one we heard in Philadelphia. At that collector's house. Remember?

**HEATHER** - How could I forget. It made you cry.

**SIMON** - Hell yes, it did! This is the same pressing. Number 126 out of 250.

**HEATHER** - So get it.

**SIMON** - Can you lend me the 400?

**HEATHER** - We're here on work-study. Earn it!

*Enter Max, the shopkeeper. He is in his sixties, bearded and artfully unkempt.*

**MAX** - Ah! And here you are. *Guten tag.*

**HEATHER** - *Guten tag. Wie getz?*

**MAX** - *Ganz gut.*

**SIMON** - Oh. Hi. Um, *ich bin sehr* ... how do I say 'impressed?'

**MAX** - ... *sehr beeindruckt. Danke.* I've been open three years now.

**SIMON** - You're American?

**MAX** - I like to think I'm international.

**SIMON** - Good thing you showed up. I was about to steal this Irena Dobos.

**MAX** - It's not worth stealing. Sorry, I didn't hear you come in. I'm Dr. Max. Not a real doctor.

**SIMON** - We're spending a semester at the St. Thomas School.

**MAX** - I know.

**HEATHER** - You do?

**SIMON** - You said this one isn't worth stealing.

**MAX** - That's right. Though if you had tried, you would have set off a proximity sensor alarm.

**SIMON** - Why bother if it's not worth ...

**MAX** - There are anti-theft tags on everything. That recording is priceless, but what you're holding is a dummy cover. The disc inside is made of plywood. I keep the real thing under lock and key. But I want people to know I carry it.

*Heather's phone rings*

**HEATHER** - *(on the phone)* Hello. Really? That's great! *(To the others)* Oh, sorry. Good news, though. They let David change his schedule. Advanced Acoustics.

**SIMON** - Remind him that the class is in German.

**HEATHER** - *(Not hearing Simon)* Yes, David. I'd say that's cause for celebration. *(a slightly shocked laugh)* Oh my God, what did you just say to me? Um ...

**SIMON** - What is it?

**HEATHER** - Nothing. Hey, David. Can I call you back?

**SIMON** - Or just tell him to get over here.

**HEATHER** - See you soon. Bye.

*Max opens cabinet and removes a copy of the Irena Dobos record.*

**MAX** - I have three copies of the Arc du Soleil pressing. But this is the one you really want.

**SIMON** - Don't tell me you have the Razmussen pressing?

**MAX** - I do. Right here. Only 100 copies were made. Pressed on 200 gram vinyl. The lathe was a custom-built Scully-Neumann with a Westrex cutting head. The master tape has since deteriorated. So this pressing is the closest thing to a mint copy you will ever find.

**SIMON** - Wow!

**HEATHER** - *(dryly)* Wow.

**MAX** - But more importantly, this pressing retains nearly the full force of the Dobos Effect. Do you know what that is?

**SIMON** - I think I do.

**MAX** - Good. Then you know it's worth the price. Eleven thousand Euros. 12 thousand American dollars. *(He extends the disc to Simon)*

**SIMON** - I'm not in the market.

**MAX** - Would you like to hear it?

**SIMON** - Sure. But, I don't want you to open it just for me.

**MAX** - I wouldn't. I've got my own copy.

**SIMON** - Oh.

**HEATHER** - We've already heard it, actually.

**SIMON** - Back in America. We went to this collector's house.

**MAX** - And he had the Razmussen pressing?

**SIMON** - No. It was the Arc de Soleil.

**MAX** - That one's nice. But it's not the Razmussen.

**SIMON** - No. I guess that must be the most valuable record in the world.

**MAX** - Not quite. An original pressing, in mint condition, would be worth a nice little fortune.

**SIMON** - Do you have that?

**MAX** - If I did, I wouldn't tell anyone.

*Heather picks up the small butterfly painting from the keyboard stand.*

**HEATHER** - Simon, look at this.

**SIMON** - A butterfly. Neat.

**MAX** - I painted that myself, a long time ago.

**SIMON** - I started painting recently.

**HEATHER** - I love butterflies. I asked him to paint me one, but he hasn't.

**SIMON** - Yet.

**MAX** - I'm out of practice myself. Let me know if you want to hear Irena. Even if you're not in the market, I'm happy to play it. Why own a 12-thousand-dollar record if you can't show it off?

**SIMON** - Yeah, I'd like that.

**MAX** - Should I play the Chaconne? It's what most people want to hear.

**HEATHER** - Watch out. It makes him emotional.

*Max chuckles*

**SIMON** - Gee, thanks, Heather.

**HEATHER** - I don't mean to embarrass you.

**MAX** - What's to be embarrassed about? It's the Dobos Effect. Papers have been written about it. People hear it and weep, or tremble, or fall in love. It's the finest recording of the most profound piece of music ever written.

**SIMON** - See?

**MAX** - Are you ready to have your mind blown? I know something not many people know. Irena recorded this in 1954, and for a long time, nobody knew exactly where the recording took place. But I found out. Care to guess?

**SIMON** - I heard it was recorded at the St. Thomas School. MAX - That's true. But where in the school?

**SIMON** - Somebody on Disc Planet posted that it in was an old rehearsal hall.

**MAX** - That was me. I post as Dr. Max.

**SIMON** - Oh! Right!

**MAX** - Now guess. Where exactly was that rehearsal hall?

**HEATHER** - Was it here?

**MAX** - *(moves a chair to a spot at center, and sets it down )* Yes! This room used to be part of the school. She stood right here.

**HEATHER** - Okay, Simon. You'd better listen to it.

**MAX** - You won't be sorry. The unusual harmonics in this recording were created on this spot, so when you play them back in this space ... well, you should brace yourself. *(To Heather)* Pull up another chair if you want.

**HEATHER** - I'm okay.

**SIMON** - I thought you liked it.

**HEATHER** - I do. But ...

**MAX** - But you've only heard the Arc du Soleil version. That one is a souvenir. The Razmussen, Simon, it's like bringing Irena Dobos back from the dead.

**HEATHER** - How do you know his name?

**MAX** - Hmm? Oh, I heard you talking. You called him Simon and you had someone named David on the phone. My apologies. I like to use first names. I hope I'm not too forward.

**HEATHER** - Okay. Whatever ... Max.

**SIMON** - Heather ...

**MAX** - It's fine. Max is my name. Max Meier. I can show you the paperwork. *(putting on record)* Are you ready?

**SIMON** - Sure.

*Simon takes off his backpack and sits in the central chair. Music begins, the opening plaintive tones of Irena's solo violin – after a few moments, Heather takes out phone and begins texting*

**SIMON** - Anything wrong?

**HEATHER** - I'm fine.

*She picks up the butterfly automaton and carries it over to the opposite side of the shop, stage left. Simon leaves his seat and goes to her. Irena's Bach Partita continues to play.*

**SIMON** - If you're bored, we don't have to stay.

**HEATHER** - No. It's not boring.

**SIMON** - So what's wrong?

**HEATHER** - He's staring at me.

**SIMON** -Really?

**HEATHER** - Really. It's very unsettling.

**SIMON** - Do you want me to say something?

**HEATHER** - I can handle it myself, thank you very much.

*A text notification sounds, Heather sets down the butterfly painting and looks at her phone.*

**HEATHER** - Listen, David wants me to help him pick something out for tomorrow night. I think I'll take off and meet up with you later.

**SIMON** - I'll come with you.

**HEATHER** - No, you should let this guy play his records for you. Just text us when you're done, okay?

**SIMON** - Yeah, okay. Sorry. I didn't want this to suck.

**HEATHER** - It doesn't. I'll see you later. *(She presses the screen of the phone, making a call.)* David? Great! Just stay right there. Pick out a place and I'll meet you in about five minutes.

*She leaves.*

# 1-B: The Shop (The Small Leap)

*Simon picks up the butterfly painting and returns to the center. He hands it to Max, then sits and continues to listen. Max puts the butterfly into the cabinet, then moves near the turntable and speaks to him.*

**MAX** - Irena Dobos. The Hungarian influence is unmistakable. Her critics felt that she took the piece too far into the countryside. But I think it's perfection. Such simplicity, and complexity. Every trip through the Chaconne brings new thoughts, new feelings. It's a mansion you can never fully explore. I'll shut up now.

*Beneath the solo violin, there is a faint bass tone that swells and then recedes. Simon begins crying, quietly. Max draws up a chair next to him.*

**MAX** - It makes you sad, because it makes you think of her. But then, so does everything. It's the Dobos Effect. You felt it when you listened to that copy at Dylan Canefield's house. It shook you. And then, out of nowhere, you felt a surge, and your emotions took over. It happened just about ... here.

*Simon is gripped by intense emotions. He begins to weep.*

**MAX** - I think we better stop, for now. *(He removes the disc, not unmoved himself. He gets a box of tissue.)* Here. We both need this.

**SIMON** - *(trying to regain control)* I'm sorry.

**MAX** - So am I. Can I get you some coffee? I have chilled cans of Café Bustelo.

**SIMON** - That's my favorite.

**MAX** - I know. Stay there. I'll get you one.

**SIMON** - How did you know about Dylan Canefield?

**MAX** - Hmm?

**SIMON** - I never said his name.

**MAX** - But you did mention that you met with a collector in Philadelphia, right?

**SIMON** - Yes.

**MAX** - Lucky guess. It's a small community. I've sold Dylan a few slabs myself. *(hands Simon the canned coffee, then picks up another album)* Mind if I lighten the mood a bit?

**SIMON** - Daft Punk?

**MAX** - Bach is divine, but there's room for some light-hearted fun. And you could use cheering up.

**SIMON** - Daft Punk doesn't cheer me up.

**MAX** - Someday it might. I used to be a snob myself.

**SIMON** - I'm not a snob.

**MAX** - You know you are.

**SIMON** - Okay, I am.

**MAX** - Feeling better?

**SIMON** - Yes.

**MAX** - I told you.

**SIMON** - I'd still rather not have ...

**MAX** - Fine. No Daft Punk. *(He puts the album away)* Silence is a rhythm too, so say The Slits. Now, to get a bit personal. The Chaconne is something that stays with you. It's yours for life. But we can't say the same for Heather Grenado.

**SIMON** - What the hell?!

**MAX** - Yes, I know her last name.

**SIMON** - You know Heather?

**MAX**- I used to, when I was younger.

**SIMON** - She said you were staring at her.

**MAX** - Guilty. I tried not to.

**SIMON** - She thought it was creepy.

**MAX** - I'm sorry. When you see her again, please apologize. I promise, I wasn't leering.

**SIMON** - How do you know her?

**MAX** - We'll get to that.

**SIMON** - This is weird.

**MAX** - It is, but you better get used to it. You're in for some quantum weirdness. I was planning on you coming in here today. I was hoping you would. I was pretty sure you would.

**SIMON** - Who are you?

**MAX** - Max Meier. Dr. Max. That's a pseudonym, but it is my legal name. I want to let you figure out exactly who I am.

**SIMON** - Am I high?

**MAX** - You don't get high. And you don't drink. And no, you haven't been drugged. Except maybe a bit by Irena Dobos and her magic violin.

**SIMON** - Okay. You have my attention. What's going on?

**MAX** - I was getting personal. You're infatuated with Heather Grenado.

**SIMON** - I'm in love with her.

**MAX** - You think so. But have it your way. You're in love with her. She doesn't feel the same way. She's fond of you. Always has been.

**SIMON** - You're starting to piss me off.

**MAX** - I would say 'get over yourself.' Cliché, but it's loaded with extra meaning in this case.

**SIMON** - What are you talking about?

**MAX** - I'm giving you a puzzle to work on. It will take your mind off of the heartache. Now, who am I? Take a close look.

**SIMON** - Are you someone I know?

**MAX** - Yes. Not well enough.

**SIMON** - Okay. You look kind of like my dad.

**MAX** - That's true. But I'm not. He's dead. Well, I don't have to tell you that.

**SIMON** - But you're family.

**MAX** - Technically. I told you, things are going to get weird. *(Takes out another album from the cabinet)* Do you know what this is?

**SIMON** - Irena Dobos. It's not ... Wow! That's not a reissue.

**MAX** - No. It's an original pressing. Mint. Any guess as to its value?

**SIMON** - Quarter million?

**MAX** - Half a million. Here, hold it.

**SIMON** - No, thanks. I can't afford the replacement fee.

**MAX** - How about if I just give it to you.

**SIMON** - You can't do that.

**MAX** - Technically true. I can't give it to you because it's already yours.

**SIMON** - Really.

**MAX** - Yes. It already belongs to Simon Lexner.

**SIMON** - Is that a clue?

**MAX** - It's a fucking giveaway. Here. Hold it.

**SIMON** - *(takes and holds it)* The cover looks brand new.

**MAX** - The man I bought it from kept it in a clean room for twenty years. It's never been played. No stylus has ever been set in its groove.

**SIMON** - *(handing it back)* You don't intend me to do it.

**MAX** - You'd have to have a really good reason. Let's stick to the Razmussen, shall we? *(puts the original back in cabinet, returns to the turntable)* Let me show you something remarkable. *(He motions for Simon to look at the Razmussen record on the turntable)* Every time you hear this recording, you feel something in your gut. The effect is strongest at two points along the groove.

**SIMON** - The null points.

**MAX** - Yes. Here and here. It happens every time. I've never experienced it with any other record. Hit that switch right there.

*Simon does – a faintly audible high-pitched sound emanates*

**MAX** - Do you hear that?

**SIMON** - It's a pilot tone.

**MAX** - You can hear it?

**SIMON** - I can feel it. It's a high-frequency carrier wave.

**MAX** - I envy you. You still have young ears. Turn that dial up, just a little – halfway between those hashmarks.

*A louder high-pitched signal, intensifying in volume*

**SIMON** - Ow!

*He turns the dial back.*

**MAX** - Not that far. It's a tone generator. I have it set up to reverberate with the harmonics of the room. Now, here's the fun part. Play the Chaconne. Let's cue it up so that it's near the first null point of the disc. When I tell you, bring up that dial. I'm not completely sure what will happen. Are you ready?

**SIMON** - Should I be?

**MAX** - Check the time. Go ahead. Look at your phone. Okay. Brace yourself. You'll feel queasy for a few seconds. It's worth it.

*Simon sets down the needle and hits the dial – there is a rumble and a high-pitched squeal – lights dim, briefly black out, then come up to reveal Heather standing by the record bin, holding the butterfly, looking at her phone, just as before. Simon groans and clutches his stomach.*

**HEATHER** - *(Startled)* - What happened?

**MAX** - Beg your pardon?

**HEATHER** - The music skipped.

**MAX** - It'll be fine.

**SIMON** - *(doubling over)* Ow! *(Noticing Heather)* What the hell.

**HEATHER** - Are you all right?

**SIMON** - Oh my God.

**MAX** - It'll pass in a moment.

*Simon goes to Heather, his arms crossed over his stomach*

**SIMON** - Did you feel that?

**HEATHER** - I heard the record skip. What's wrong?

**SIMON** - Um, nothing? *(He looks at Max. Max makes an indication to his wrist.)* What time do you have?

**HEATHER** - *(Sets down butterfly and looks at phone)* Three thirty-two.

**SIMON** - Holy shit. *(He looks at Max, who gives an "I told you so" gesture with his hands)* Are you all right?

**HEATHER** - He's staring at me.

**SIMON** - Yes. He is. I ... don't think he means anything ...

**HEATHER** - It's very unsettling.

*A notification tone from Heather's phone. She begins to text.*

**HEATHER** - Listen, David wants me to help him pick something out for tomorrow night. I think I'll take off and meet up with you later.

**SIMON** - I ... I really think I should come with you.

**HEATHER** - No! No, you should let this guy play his records for you. Just text us when you're done, okay?

**SIMON** - Yeah. Okay.

*Heather makes a call.*

**HEATHER** - David? Great! Just stay right there. Pick out a place and I'll meet you in about five minutes. *(She exits)*

# 1-C: The Shop (Preparation)

**SIMON** - What the fuck just happened.

**MAX** - *(removing stylus from record)* I told you it was weird.

**SIMON** - Was that a... time jump?

**MAX** - It sure was. Triggered by a combination of harmonics, geographic alignment, and a quirk in the Dobos recording that you discovered. Or I discovered. It's one hell of an anomaly.

**SIMON** - No. I'm not ... you're not ... *(he begins crying)*

**MAX** - Fine. You've had a shock. And this really is just the tip of the proverbial iceberg. Oh, come on! You're blubbering. It's pathetic.

**SIMON** - Shut the hell up!

**MAX** - You think I don't know what you're feeling? I know it to an exactitude. To be blunt, she doesn't love you. She never will.

**SIMON** - Yeah, I just now figured that out. It's become incredibly obvious who she loves.

**MAX** - That's right. David Caro. You've known it for some time. You've been suppressing it. But now it's hit you over the head and you can't deny it. Sucks, but it's nothing special. Happens to just about everyone. Follow the wise counsel of Elsa and Let It Go.

**SIMON** - I hate that song!

**MAX** - I know.

**SIMON** - Augh! You keep saying that!

**MAX** - You keep missing the obvious!

**SIMON** - I give up! You need to tell me what's going on.

**MAX** - I think you know. *(Picks retrieves the butterfly painting and takes it to Simon)* Here. Look at it closely. *(Simon does)* I began painting when I was a sophomore in high school. I wasn't half bad. I particularly liked small watercolors This one is special. Do you know why?

**SIMON** - No.

**MAX** - Because you painted it. You, yourself. You made it for Heather. Look at the signature.

**SIMON** - When?

**MAX** - About a year and a half from now. How badly do you need me to spell this out?

**SIMON** - *(Stunned)* I've leapt through time.

**MAX** - You jumped back a few minutes. I've jumped farther than that. A few times. Not very many.

**SIMON** - I'm talking to myself.

**MAX** - Fuckin' A! Hope you're ready for the prize. *(Simon collapses into chair, not a faint, just a helpless collapse)* Hey! Careful. Don't drop that. *(He takes the painting from Simon)*

**SIMON** - This isn't real.

**MAX** - I know this is hard. You just looked in a mirror and saw this ugly old mug. Yes, Simon, I'm you. I'm sixty-four. You still need me, you'll still feed me, right?

**SIMON** - *(beginning to withdraw)* I can't handle this.

**MAX** - You can. I'm going to make handling it a little easier for you. I hope.

*Simon draws his arms up near his head and brings his legs up onto the seat, trying to escape by curling up into an embryonic ball.*

**SIMON** - *(muttering, then screaming)* No no no no no ... NO! NO!

*Max hands him another can of coffee.*

**MAX** - I hate to add caffeine to your panic, but I know it'll help. *(Simon calms down enough to accept the can)* Focus on the deliciousness. And yes, it is good. I went for years without it. Now I have it shipped to me. *(Simon drinks)* Good. Let the flavor wash away the weirdness and the heartbreak. The shock is over. It's all daisies and churros from here.

**SIMON** - I'm all right now.

*He sniffles and then wipes his nose with his hand. Max hands him a handkerchief.*

**MAX** - Please use this. Now, I said there was a prize for guessing who I am. It's a doozy. The rarest, most valuable record in the world. Now, you have to be a little bit curious, yes?

*Simon finishes off the can*

**SIMON** - I don't like you very much.

**MAX** - Sure, you find 'old you' disturbing. I find 'young me' embarrassing. Don't think of us as one person. Because we're not. I mean, up to a point, we're identical. But there's a place in time where we divide. I have a lot of history that you don't. I want to bring you up to date, fill you in on where you've been all these years. It's important.

**SIMON** - You're changing time.

**MAX** - Yes. Deliberately. Ready to hear my story?

**SIMON** - *(quietly)* Go ahead.

**MAX** - When I was twenty-two, when I was you, I flew from Philadelphia to Leipzig with my two best friends, Heather and David. We had a week to explore the city before we started our studies. As you know, I was in the middle of the worst crush of my life, an obsession, really. It had been going on for two years. Unhealthy. But it happens to a lot of people. Right?

**SIMON** - Sure.

**MAX** - I was about to study acoustical physics in a city of exquisite music. I knew that during the program, I would engineer recordings in St. Thomas Church, a privilege that thrilled me to the core. So far, so much in common. *(Max goes to keyboard and plays introductory theme for the Bach Chaconne)* You've met Dr. Shosen. He already knows about the Dobos Effect. If you ask him about it next week, he will tell you that it gives him a feeling of discorporation, a momentary out-of-body rush.

I told Doctor Shosen I wanted to figure out why the Dobos record had this remarkable property. I learned every note of the Chaconne. I studied all of Bach, but with special attention to the partitas. Edifying, of course. But not a clue about the special weirdness of the Dobos record. By mid- semester, the mystery remained. So I brought David to the lab. I played the record for him.

**SIMON** - He's heard it.

**MAX** - He's heard the CD. I played him the vinyl. It lit him up. It became as much of a cause for him as for me.

**SIMON** - Oh my God. Of course. David and his Physics.

**MAX** - Yes. You and I are smart, well above average. David is in his own category.

**SIMON** - Did he figure it out? Did he leave any notes?

**MAX** - Slow down. I will reveal everything. David and I spent two semesters here. Heather went home after just one.

**SIMON** - Really.

**MAX** - She got tired of our constant shoptalk. David and I got lost in the project. We worked late, slept in the lab. She felt like a third wheel, so she went home.

**SIMON** - And that was it for Heather and David?

**MAX** - Hardly. Distance only intensified their feelings. But for you, I mean for me, with Heather gone, I was able to focus on my work. I made test recordings.

I had the best violin students play the Chaconne. In the process, I became a hell of a recording engineer. But I couldn't reproduce the Dobos effect. I could only examine it.

**SIMON** - But David solved it.

**MAX** - *(nodding)* He noticed that the effect is stronger at certain times of day. And four times a year, the graph showed a consistent peak. The effect is most powerful at ...

**SIMON** - At the solstices and equinoxes.

**MAX** - Right. Good intuition. David cracked the numbers. He found the anomaly. On those specific days, the math just wouldn't come out right. According to David, the only way to make sense of his data was to infer a temporal disruption. A slight blip in space-time.

**SIMON** - When did you make the first jump?

**MAX** - We made a breakthrough at the end of our second semester. By then we had learned about this room and talked the owner into letting us work here. The tone generator was my idea. It was a lucky guess.

**SIMON** - But it worked.

**MAX** - Technically. It wasn't much of a leap. Less than a minute. And it was painful. We both suffered physical symptoms. David was sick for more than a week. But our clocks told the story. We really did it.

**SIMON** - Right here?

**MAX** - Yes. Shook the place up pretty good. It cracked that window. I had to invent a story about a drunken fellow student to explain it away.

**SIMON** - It's not broken now.

**MAX** - Of course not. Because it hasn't happened yet.

**SIMON** - Oh right. And so you both went time traveling.

**MAX** - No. That test scared the hell out of us. David went back to the States. I stayed here for a while longer, then I returned to Philadelphia myself. I'm sure you know why.

**SIMON** - No, I don't.

**MAX** - I couldn't stand being on the other side of the ocean knowing that he was with Heather. So I went back and I pretended to be happy for them. I acted like I was over it. I was their best friend, content to be unrequited. Just so I could be near her. So if they ever separated, I would be there to swoop in. I was an idiot.

**SIMON** - Okay, I get your point.

**MAX** - Do you? Because it took me a very long time to get it. I built myself a customized private Hell in Philadelphia. But never mind. I knew that one day I would have to come back to Leipzig. I had a grand plan. Thinking about it helped to distract me.

**SIMON** - What grand plan.

**MAX** - What if I use this room to step through time? What if I could create an impossible record? The music of Johann Sebastian Bach, played by Johann Sebastian Bach in the sanctuary of St. Thomas Church. The best use of time travel I could think of.

**SIMON** - Oh my God. Have you done it?

**MAX** - One step at a time. What matters is that the plan sustained me. Without it, I wouldn't be talking to you now. I'd be dead, Simon. I hate to keep pounding a drum you don't want to hear. But obsessive love, which is what you have, it's destructive. I hope you get to grips with that sooner than I did.

*Simon is silent.*

**MAX** - So eventually I dropped out of school and moved back here to Leipzig. I changed my name to Max Meier.

**SIMON** - Why?

**MAX** - Because Simon Lexner became a lost cause, a toxic person. I couldn't stand to be him anymore. Max Meier was able to put the grand plan into action. Here in Liepzig, I picked up recording gigs. Made decent money. And I leased this place.

*Lights dim. During the next bit of narration, Simon exits in darkness.*

**MAX** - At first I told myself that it was just a mental exercise. I needed that. A grand puzzle to figure out. This room gave me the key. It dates back to 1712. We're almost to the best part, Simon.

*He crosses to the cabinet and removes the Dr. Max sign.*

This cabinet was already here. It's as old as the building itself. Older. And it's been here from day one. I hope you can understand the significance of that. A container of continuity.

*Simon reenters as young Max in the flashback timeline and acts out the next bit of narration as older Max relates it. He now wears different clothes, a jacket and black shirt.*

The cabinet jumped before I ever did. My first test, I emptied it out, and I adjusted the triangulation to cover that back half of the room. I set the harmonics and put the turntable on autoplay. Then I went outside. When the stylus hit the null point, the whole building shook. There was a soft kind of plasma. I saw it drift through the glass of the windows and even seep through the bricks and mortar.

*Simon exits and the null point plays. The turntable sparks and smokes, then stops. Simon returns and opens the cabinet. It contains a clarinet, an oboe, and some stacks of sheet music. He removes them and looks at them in astonishment.*

It was a moment of triumph. Physical objects from at least two hundred years ago, translated from one time-plane to another. Intact and showing no signs of age. I knew then that I would make the attempt, and that I stood at least some chance of success.

*Simon exits and returns with a dolly carrying two small crates, which he loads into the cabinet.*

Better still, the cabinet would allow me to take the equipment I'd need. I bought a refurbished TEAC reel to reel tape machine. A dozen reels of blank tape. On one of them, I copied the Razmussen at high speed, as a possible means of trying to get back.

I took the best small speakers I could afford, a preamplifier, three battery packs. Four solar-powered chargers. Through testing, I found that I could power the tape machine for two hours, and recharge it in 36, weather permitting.

I packed three Telefunken U-47 microphones, with the cables and power packs to connect them. In the left lower drawer, I placed a tone generator. A few odds and ends. I bundled a Walkman, batteries, a few books, a few snacks. Three cans of coffee. And I brought the painting I had made for Heather. It's been backward and forward too.

I no longer had David's expertise. But I checked and double-checked the math, and I waited for the Autumn equinox.

*Simon sets the platter on the turntable.*

And the day arrived.

*Music begins, then a rumble, then flashes of bright light. Simon falls into a heap, clutching his gut, and screaming in agony*

The process hurts. You felt some nausea going back a few minutes. Imagine the pain of leaping centuries. To be honest, I didn't expect to survive. Part of me didn't want to.

# 1-D: An Apartment in Leipzig

*The lights go out entirely. After a silence, the light of an oil lantern is seen flickering, then setting down onto a covered table. A hand turns up the lamp. Katarina, in 18th century dress, moves over to a chair, where Simon sits back, asleep.*

**KATARINA** - Is anyone alive?

*Lights Up – There is no sign of the record shop. The drapings and props indicate a much earlier time period. Simon remains unresponsive.*

**KATARINA** - Is anyone alive today? You're breathing, but that's about all.

*She takes up a basin and cloth and begins washing his face with it. Simon's eyes open.*

**KATARINA** - Oh! Ulbrecht! Uli! Come quick!

*Uli enters quickly*

**ULI** - What is it?

**KATARINA** - He's opened his eyes!

**ULI** - Good. Good! Go tell the doctor!

**KATARINA** - *(to Simon)* Can you see us? Are you able to speak?

**ULI** - Don't test him, Katarina. Just go for the doctor.

**KATARINA** - Of course. *(She exits)*

**ULI** - *(to Simon)* Can you see us? Are you able to speak?

**SIMON** - *(whispering)* Guten abend. Good evening?

**ULI** - We didn't know whether to take you to the surgeons or to the jail.

**SIMON** - Jail?

**ULI** - You were very drunk.

**SIMON** - No. No, I don't drink.

**ULI** - Don't you.

**SIMON** - No. Well ... coffee.

**ULI** - Ah! Coffee. There's your vice, then.

**SIMON** - Not drunk. Just very sick.

**ULI** - I see. That would also explain the puking.

**SIMON** - I'm very sorry. I don't remember.

**ULI** - You're lucky Katarina was at my side when I found you. She is tender-hearted. I would never have taken such pity. Do you feel all right?

**SIMON** - No. Not really. Please, where am I?

**ULI** - An apartment at the student commons, but it's empty right now. We use it for visiting lecturers.

**SIMON** - Leipzig Academy? St. Thomas School?

**ULI** - Yes. So you know it.

**SIMON** - By reputation. It's the very place I wanted to go.

**ULI** - So it appears. We found you in one of our rehearsal chambers. I summoned the constable. When he came on the scene, you had ceased vomiting and fallen unconscious. If it was up to me, you would have spent the night in jail. But Katarina spoke up for you. She told the constable she guessed you were a student, and as nothing had been stolen, she agreed to look after you. I think her foolish, and I count the constable an even greater fool to have agreed.

**SIMON** - Thank you. I deserved the jail.

**ULI** - You're not German.

**SIMON** - No. I'm from Philadelphia.

**ULI** - The British Colonies?

**SIMON** - Oh. Yes. Of course.

**ULI** - What is your business in Leipzig?

**SIMON** - Music.

*He tries to stand and collapses on the floor. Lights out. Max appears in spotlight to continue narrating.*

**MAX** - I learned that the year was 1744. I spent two nights in a hospital, wracked with fever and internal pain. They treated the fever with a tincture of Jesuit's Bark from Peru. It's quinine. They just didn't have a name for it yet. For the pain, I was given laudanum. Opium mixed with brandy. I know you'll be disappointed to find out that I really liked it.

*Lights up – Simon is bare chested. Uli brings him a simple white shirt.*

**ULI** - I trust you are well.

**SIMON** - Much better.

**ULI** - Wear this. If you feel strong enough, I've been asked to bring you back to the apartments at the academy.

**SIMON** - *(putting on shirt)* I think I am. Thank you.

**ULI** - I am perturbed, young man. Perhaps you can put my mind at ease. First thing. Who are you?

**SIMON** - My name is Max Meier.

**ULI** - You have no papers, no identification.

**SIMON** - No. I've lost them.

**ULI** - So, Max Meier from Philadelphia. You say you have traveled all the way to Leipzig for the music.

**SIMON** - Yes.

**ULI** - Herr Meier, you have a German name. Have you got family here?

**SIMON** - Not that I know of. Not anymore. My forbears immigrated to America a long time ago.

**ULI** - How long ago?

**SIMON** - I don't really know. I came here because this is where my studies have led me. I've told you who I am. May I know your name?

**ULI** - Falkenrath.

**SIMON** - Falkenrath! I like that.

**ULI** - I'm not concerned with you liking it. I am an administrator for the St. Thomas School, charged with running its dormitories and keeping order among the resident students. It seems that, with no permission, you broke into Practice Hall Number 12.

**SIMON** - No, I didn't break in. I'm afraid I can't explain how I got there. ULI - You don't remember?

**SIMON** - I came to Leipzig, and I just ... found myself there. Oh! Of course. You must have seen my belongings.

**ULI** - I did not.

**SIMON** - They're in the practice hall.

**ULI** - Are they.

**SIMON** - All right, yes, I entered the room on purpose. I saw that large cabinet. I hid all of my belongings in it. I can only hope they haven't been stolen.

**ULI** - But, Herr Meier, why would you do such a thing ...

**SIMON** - I confess, Herr Falkenrath. I brought some unusual things with me. I'm a scientist. I have equipment that would be difficult to explain to a layman.

**ULI** - What kind of scientist?

**SIMON** - Of sound. I study acoustics. I have equipment that helps me to analyze sound waves. My aim is to study the harmonics of St. Thomas Church. I promise you, it was my aim to contact the school and explain my project to them.

**ULI** - And the instruments of your science are hidden in Practice Hall 12.

**SIMON** - I hope so.

**ULI** - I will go there now. And then, Herr Meier, it will be my duty to report this unorthodox entry of yours to the Burgomaster. Be ready to tell him the truth. For now, come with me. I am under orders from my fiancé.

# 1-E: A Parlor at St. Thomas Academy

*Katarina enters and sets out tea and biscuits – lights shift to indicate change of location.*

**KATARINA** - Welcome back, Herr Meier. I'm glad to see you looking well.

**SIMON** - Thank you, Miss ...

**KATARINA** - Call me Katarina.

**SIMON** - You live here?

**KATARINA** - I work here. But yes, I spend so much time, I might as well say that I live here. We have a hundred students, with a thousand problems to attend to.

**SIMON** - Sorry to have added to your troubles.

**KATARINA** - You didn't ask to catch fever. But I'm pleased that you've recovered.

**SIMON** - I'm afraid I've made myself very conspicuous. I didn't mean to.

**KATARINA** - Uli tells me you are some kind of secret scientist.

**SIMON** - I'm doing research. It needs to be confidential, for now.

**KATARINA** - Are you sure you're not a spy?

**SIMON** - I would be a very poor spy.

**KATARINA** - So, why Leipzig, Herr Meier? If music is your interest, why not Vienna?

**SIMON** - Leipzig has a fine reputation. But I chose it for St. Thomas Church. And for its Cantor. Are you acquainted with Herr Bach? Johann Sebastian Bach?

**KATARINA** - *(laughing)* I know him better than most. He's my father.

**MAX** - All of my calculations had been crude guesses. Just the same, I had landed exactly where and when I needed to be. Katarina arranged for her father to join us the next evening. She also found some clothes better suited to my new surroundings.

*Katarina gives Simon a coat, not ornate, but appropriately dignified. He puts it on.*

**KATARINA** - I don't know what they wear in Philadelphia, Herr Meier, but with this coat, you at least look presentable. I don't mean to offend.

**SIMON** - You are only saying what's true.

**KATARINA** - I didn't know what to tell Papa about you. He's awfully curious.

*Enter Johann Sebastian Bach*

**BACH** - Katarina Dorothea!

**KATARINA** - Papa.

**BACH** - And this is our visitor from across the ocean.

**SIMON** - Maxwell Meier. It is an incredible honor, Herr Bach.

**BACH** - You mean to say that I am known in the British Colonies?

**SIMON** - Yes! Very much so.

**BACH** - By virtue of my reputation as organist?

**SIMON** - As a composer. I first heard your work at a church in Philadelphia. They had an ensemble playing your Brandenburg Concertos. It was delightful.

**BACH** - My what?

**SIMON** - The concerti you submitted to Christian-Ludwig in Brandenburg.

**KATARINA** - Have I heard these, Papa?

**BACH** - Nobody has! I'm not aware that those works ever left Herr Ludwig's file drawer.

**SIMON** - Ah. Yes. Well … they have. I've examined the scores myself. BACH - Herr Meier, we have just met, and I'm not in the habit of calling men liars. But I do not believe you.

**SIMON** - I understand. I don't know how to explain it.

**BACH** - Don't explain. Play.

**SIMON** - Play?

**BACH** - *(indicating to keyboard, now draped to represent a harpsichord)* You say you've examined these scores. Demonstrate it. Play me any sixteen bars.

**SIMON** - I'm no musician, Herr Bach. I barely passed my piano proficiencies. But I'll try.

*He sits down and plays the intro to the first concerto, just well enough that the melody is recognizable.*

**BACH** - You are right.

**SIMON** - Yes. I really have heard them.

**BACH** - I mean you are right, you cannot play.

**SIMON** - No, Herr Bach. I insult your music. I'm clumsy. And a little nervous at the moment.

**BACH** - Why be nervous? You've just made me very happy indeed. Happy and angry. I had no idea those scores had gone abroad. Leave it to Christian-Ludwig! Never a reply in twenty years. And yet, it has been played. In Philadelphia. This is the most remarkable thing I have ever heard.

**KATARINA** - Played and appreciated, I'm sure.

**SIMON** - More than appreciated. A standing ovation.

**BACH** - In a church?

**SIMON** - A public concert in the sanctuary, not during services.

**BACH** - Was it a Lutheran church?

**SIMON** - Anglican.

**BACH** - Of course. And you must be Anglican?

**SIMON** - Episcopal. Yes. That's the church I was raised in.

**BACH** - You no longer attend?

**SIMON** - No. I don't recognize any church, or creed. I have no religion.

**BACH** - None?

**SIMON** - Only music. Everything else is division and war. Religion is brutality. Music alone is divine.

**BACH** - My God, Katarina. You've brought into these halls a genuine radical. This, I put it to you, is nothing less than a young man in the grip of Enlightenment.

**SIMON** - I hope you aren't troubled.

**BACH** - Ha! You must meet my oldest son, Carl Phillip. He is in Prussia, employed at the court of Frederick the Great. Now there is the very essence of your Enlightenment, yes?

**SIMON** - Frederick is an imposing figure.

**BACH** - Perhaps you will join me when I go to meet him. I'm sure he would find your ideas highly stimulating.

**SIMON** - I think I might strain the limits of his tolerance. And yours.

**BACH** - Mine? I am famously tolerant. I have entertained beggars and bandits, tax collectors and revolutionaries. They may say whatever they like. I only lose my temper if they attack the Art.

**KATARINA** - Or boast after playing badly.

**BACH** - You aren't bringing up that matter of the bassoon again, are you?

**KATARINA** - It seems fair to warn him, Papa.

**BACH** - Katarina is worried that I might instigate another street fight. It happened only once, but it seems I will never live it down. Early in my career, I was engaged at Arnstadt. One night, a student by the name of Geyersbach came chasing after me, wielding a stick, shouting that I had insulted him.

**SIMON** - Had you?

**BACH** - No! It was Geyersbach who insulted me, with his bassoon. With his ghastly intonation and lack of rhythmic sense, I believe he insulted everyone at that evening's serenade. I said as much, publicly. So, the young man waited in a dark alley. I strolled by, smoking an evening pipe, and with a yell, he was upon me. He struck me across the face with his hand, then raised his cudgel.

**SIMON** - What did you do?

**BACH** - What any man of sense would do. I drew my knife! He leaped at me, and with my blade, I caught hold of his jacket. Then we both tumbled to the ground, and next I knew, a constable had me by the collar.

**KATARINA** - He nearly lost his post.

**BACH** - But there were witnesses. Everyone saw that he struck me first. And I am satisfied to report that the wretchedness of his playing was set down in court as a matter of public record.

**SIMON** - As I said, I'm no musician.

**BACH** - Ulbrecht tells me you are a scientist of music.

**SIMON** - Yes. Acoustics. Harmonics. These are the sciences that make the art possible.

*Reenter Uli*

**BACH** - Intriguing. Let's lift a glass, then.

**ULI** - I think you'll find that Herr Meier does not drink.

**BACH** - No?

**ULI** -So he told us.

**BACH** - This is the most astonishing thing of all! A man raised in the Episcopal Church who does not drink!

**KATARINA** - We can bring you tea.

**ULI** - Or coffee.

**SIMON** - Yes. Coffee.

**BACH** - Ah I've written a cantata about coffee. Raised a few eyebrows.
**SIMON** - I think of it as fuel. My work keeps me up long hours.

**BACH** - As does mine. My natural inclination is to stay awake for too long, and so I take brandy of an evening. Otherwise, I might see the sunrise before I've put down my quill.

**KATARINA** - Father works too hard.

**BACH** - If my request for a raise were to be granted, Katarina, I might afford some leisure. For now, I must content myself with the occasional sustained rest. *(He traces a fermata in the air)*

**ULI** - Ha! I get it! Sustained rest.

**BACH** - You see? My oldest daughter has waited a long time to marry, but she has found a man of quick wit.

**ULI** - I believe Herr Bach is using sarcasm.

**KATARINA** - It's a very old joke, Ulbrecht.

**SIMON** - But a good one. My congratulations, Herr Falkenrath. I hope you will both be very happy.

**BACH** - With many children.

**KATARINA** - Papa, you know very well that isn't ...

**BACH** - Isn't possible? Nonsense. I have sired twenty children. Your sister Regina is only two years old. Anna gave birth to her at the age of forty-one. So it is never too late for either of you. Look at me, I am almost sixty.

**KATARINA** - (mortified) Oh, Papa.

**BACH** - It's nothing to be embarrassed about. Just because I dedicate my life to glorifying God does not mean I take orders like some poor abbot. The Lord has blessed me with a prodigious regenerative inclination. I praise him for it.

**KATARINA** - I'm starting to think this isn't your first brandy tonight.

**BACH** - Of course not. It's my third. And last. Not enough to cause inebriation. Just enough to relax the mind and mortify my children. (rises) But I think I am wearing on my daughter's hospitality. Herr Meier, it has been a great pleasure to meet you. I wish you all good fortune with your work. Now, there is a bed waiting not far from here, and a good woman whose virtues deserve their own sonatas. Good night, young man.

*Katarina sees her father out as Uli approaches Simon.*

**ULI** - A word with you, Herr Meier. I have inspected the items you hid in the cabinet of the practice hall.

**SIMON** - Yes?

**ULI** - You meant it when you said they were unusual. I couldn't give a name to a single thing I saw there.

**SIMON** - I know.

**ULI** - Would these machines be more familiar to people in Philadelphia?

**SIMON** - No. There is nothing like them anywhere else in the world.

**ULI** - You must have some financial support for this science.

**SIMON** - I've funded it all myself. I once had extravagant means, it's true. Not anymore. I'm down to a couple of ducats.

**ULI** - I'm torn, Herr Meier. On the one hand, it's a scandal that I haven't already reported you. On the other, I'd be lying if I didn't admit that I'm curious.

**SIMON** - I'm in no position to ask for more favors. But if you help me to keep a low profile, I could share some of my work.

**ULI** - That puts me at some risk, Herr Maier. I expect you to answer my every question. In return, I will see that Practice Hall 12 is kept off limits to the students. You will have your own key. Be sure that if I have any occasion for alarm or concern, I will do my duty and alert the town officials. Am I understood?

**SIMON** - Yes, Herr Falkenrath.

**ULI** - My silence in exchange for full disclosure. I want to see what those machines do. I want you to explain them to me.

**SIMON** - I ... I don't know if I can.

**ULI** - You think I'm too dull?

**SIMON** - No. But I think you will find it unsettling.

**ULI** - I don't care. I've stated my terms. I'm protecting the interests of this school, and of the family I am about to marry into. Do you understand that?

**SIMON** - Of course.

**ULI** - Then we're settled. I hope we may begin soon.

# 1-F: In the Loft at St. Thomas Church

*Lights shift – colored patterns suggesting stained glass indicate transition to church interior – Johann Sebastian Bach approaches and sits at the keyboard, the sound of the St. Thomas pipe organ is heard playing an organ prelude – Simon enters quietly as Bach practices. Bach notices and stops.*

**BACH** - Is somebody here?

**SIMON** - I'm sorry, Herr Bach. It's only me.

**BACH** - Herr Meier. I was expecting my student, Altnickol. Are you here for instruction? You need it.

**SIMON** - I would never want to waste your time.

**BACH** - You would not waste my time. I would have Altnickol teach you. He is one of my best students.

**SIMON** - He's fortunate to learn from someone of your eminence.

**BACH** - No, no! You speak as if I was some kind of archangel. You may love the art, but never idolize the wretches who make that art.

**SIMON** - You are no wretch.

**BACH** - I'm a servant, Herr Meier. I carry out my duty to the church and to my patrons. In return, I am paid far too little. Now, how may I be of service to you?

**SIMON** - I came to Leipzig to conduct a study of the acoustics of this church. More than that, I aim to capture the acoustics during the performance of its music.

**BACH** - Capture?

**SIMON** - Yes. I have instruments that I wish to place here, in three carefully chosen spots. When you play the organ, or when your choir sings, this equipment will actually respond to the musical vibrations, and capture the data I need.

**BACH** - You mean to say that after a performance, you can examine it.

**SIMON** - Scientifically. Yes.

**BACH** - And you have set up in Practice Hall 12 for this effort.

**SIMON** - Yes.

**BACH** - My students call it the Haunted Hall. For years, there has been talk of strange vibrations, of living shadows and ghosts. Even you, Herr Maier, seem to have appeared quite suddenly in that room. Perhaps you are a ghost.

**SIMON** - I assure you, I am flesh and blood.

**BACH** - Of course you are. I was attempting a joke. But there is something odd about you.

**SIMON** - Even in my home country, nobody would dispute that.

**BACH** - Odd but bright, yes? Herr Falkenrath tells me you bring strange instruments to do this work. I fear this might be a distraction to our congregants. This is a house of God.

**SIMON** - I don't propose to conduct my study during worship. But during rehearsal. The parish office said I needed your approval.

**BACH** - Then I will ask you a question. My permission depends upon your answer.

**SIMON** - Very well.

*Bach plays a brief organ passage*

**BACH** - This instrument. Is it equally tempered or is it well-tempered?
SIMON - To my ear, it is neither. It is pure intonation.

**BACH** - Very good. You are qualified to answer my true question. Would you prefer my cantata be accompanied on the organ as it is currently tuned, or would you prefer to hear it from a tempered organ?

**SIMON** - Tempered, Herr Bach.

**BACH** - You didn't even hesitate.

**SIMON** - No, sir.

**BACH** - Even-temperament is a compromise of the natural order.

**SIMON** - Yes. And that compromise opens the door to modulations, transpositions, to an infinite variety of harmonic inventions.

**BACH** - Thank you! Would you please talk to Herr Silbermann!

**SIMON** - Who is he?

**BACH** - The man who built this organ. He insists on keeping this barbaric tuning, which assaults the ear of man and God. Can you use your science to show him the possibilities of a well-tempered tuning?

**SIMON** - I am sure he would be astonished.

**BACH** - Then you have my permission to turn this sanctuary upside down if it will bring me justice!

# 1-G: The Shop (1st Interlude)

*A swelling of choral music- Gloria in Excelsis Deo from the B Minor Mass, BWV 191 – Max is revealed to be playing it on the turntable in the present. Simon rejoins in his 21st century attire, and takes a seat, listening attentively.*

**MAX** - It was too easy. Within days, I was placing microphones in the sanctuary and recording the chancery choir. The result is on sale right here in the shop. You've already held a copy.

**SIMON** - The Arcturus Ensemble?

**MAX** - That's right. I pressed a thousand of them when I got back. I don't think I've sold even ten.

**SIMON** - Maybe if people knew what it really was.

*Max takes off the record*

**MAX** - How could I ever convince anyone to believe it? Still, it delights me to know that a handful of people have in their possession an actual recording of Johann Bach playing and conducting his own chorale. Available for the low price of fourteen dollars. It's all about perceived value in this world.

**SIMON** - Why did you call them the Arcturus Ensemble?

**MAX** - Our middle name is Arthur.

**SIMON** - Ah! Of course.

**MAX** - It's the fourth brightest star in the sky, and the first one I saw when I returned from the past.

**SIMON** - I should call Heather and let her know where I am.

**MAX** - Don't bother. You'll notice she hasn't been asking.

*Simon glances at his phone*

**SIMON** - True.

**MAX** - I have a good idea of where they are, based on my own painful experience. But it doesn't matter anymore, right? Please tell me it seems less important to you.

**SIMON** - Of course it's important to me.

**MAX** - Sure, but less important.

**SIMON** - Less important than the fact that I'm going to jump through time? Yeah, I guess it is.

**MAX** - Hang on! Nobody ever said a thing about you making a time jump. I'm not telling you my story so that you can repeat my mistakes.

**SIMON** - I just meant, I'm you, and ...

**MAX** - *(with sudden force)* You're not me! Not anymore. And you should be goddamn grateful.

**SIMON** - Why? Did something go wrong? I mean, you came back.

**MAX** - You'll understand soon enough. *(regaining composure)* Do you want a copy of this? I'm happy to throw it in.

**SIMON** - Sure. *(begins texting)*

**MAX** - You're not going to bring them here, are you?

**SIMON** - No. I'm not. Look.

**MAX** - (reading his text) "Don't wait up for me. Have a good night." Excellent choice, Simon.

**SIMON** - In case you're wondering, I haven't magically stopped caring.

**MAX** - I don't expect you to. I'm just trying to lay the groundwork.

**SIMON** - For?

**MAX** - A better future. I'm hungry. Are you? There's some good Indian takeout across the street.

**SIMON** - Not for me. I'm still a little queasy.

**MAX** - How's your sense of reality? This is a lot to take in.

**SIMON** - You don't say.

**MAX** - I'm breaking this as gently as I can. I don't want to overwhelm you.

**SIMON** - When did you find out about David?

**MAX** - What about him?

**SIMON** - When did you discover the two of them were a thing.

**MAX** - Tomorrow morning. Day three of our stay in Leipzig

**SIMON** - How did you find out?

**MAX** - They told me. We had breakfast at Café Corso.

**SIMON** - Yeah. We're still planning on that.

**MAX** - Don't go. It'll suck. They'll break it to you in the nicest way they can, because they know how you feel. The kinder they are, the more condescending it will seem. You will end up embarrassed and hurt. So spare yourself.

**SIMON** - Maybe you haven't gotten over it.

**MAX** - I have. I do admit, seeing her again after four decades, it was uncanny. I know I was staring. It brought back memories. And I'd just as soon do without them. I really made an ass of myself over her. I bought her things, I painted pictures. I even wrote songs for her.

**SIMON** - Any good?

**MAX** - No. Terrible. They've vanished forever through a fold in spacetime. And there they will stay. I forbid you to write any songs! Ever!

**SIMON** - What should I do?

**MAX** - Nothing! Leave it alone. You don't love her. You don't really know her. Your brain is doping you up, making you feel like a tormented romantic hero. Don't let the obsession control you.

**SIMON** - It's not an obsession.

**MAX** - You wanna bet? Even now you're preoccupied with it, despite the fact that you're talking to your older self in a record store that houses a time warp and vinyl recordings of J.S. Fucking Bach!

**SIMON** - Point taken.

**MAX** - Bottle that angst and put a label on it. Toxic Hormonal Bullshit. Done?

**SIMON** - If you say so.

**MAX** - I want you to hear something.

*He puts on another record – a boy soprano singing 'et exultavit' from the Magnificat*

MAX - You know it?

SIMON - The Magnificat.

*He slips into shadow as Max continues talking.*

**MAX** - The D minor version. I got permission to run my tests during a rehearsal. I think I captured the sanctuary space quite nicely. This is the first tape I let Uli listen to. Even played back on small speakers, the performance really came to life.

# 1-H: Practice Hall 12

*Transition back to 18th century. Uli is listening, astonished, as the tape reels spin. Simon-as-young-Max enters.*

**SIMON** - You see? I wasn't making things up.

**ULI** - I don't know what to say. This is miraculous.

**SIMON** - It's just science. Clever tricks using natural laws. *(He turns off the tape)*

**ULI** - What do you intend to do with these?

**SIMON** - Save them. Preserve them. Hundreds of years from now, people can listen and feel as if they've gone back to an earlier time.

**ULI** - But ... don't you see? This will change the world.

**SIMON** - Yes. I know it will, in time.

**ULI** - I mean now. Have you no idea what men would pay? Noblemen could have Faustina performing on command while they sit on their privies. There's a fortune to be made here.

**SIMON** - No. Don't even start down this road, Uli. I swore you to secrecy.

**ULI** - I know.

**SIMON** - Tell nobody about these recordings. It's crucial.

**ULI** - But they're amazing.

**SIMON** - Just trust me when I say the world isn't ready for this. Be glad you got to hear it, then forget about it, all right?

**ULI** - Of course. I keep my word, Max.

**SIMON** - I believe you.

**ULI** - But one person. Please let me tell Katarina.

**SIMON** - No, Uli. Nobody.

**ULI** - It's just that ... all right, no. Never mind.

**SIMON** - Whatever that thought was, put it away.

**ULI** - But Max, what if you hide this? Place the receptors, the ...

**SIMON** - Microphones.

**ULI** - Microphones. You could hide them in the chambers where emperors and generals make their plans. You could turn the tides of war.

**SIMON** - By spying. Yes, that application has been thought of, Uli. You've seen how much work it is to set this up. You'd be caught.

**ULI** - But this ... you would have their very words, unfiltered by faulty memory or personal bias. An utterly perfect field report from enemy headquarters. Imagine it!

**SIMON** - Uli, this is not a machine for war! This is for art.

**ULI** - Or for the defense of art, Max. It's only a matter of time before there's another fight for control of our borders. This could save us.

**SIMON** - That's exactly the kind of thinking I want to avoid. I am only here to capture a few sacred choruses. That's it. And when my purpose is done, I'm going to disappear, and you'll never see me again. That's how it has to be.

**ULI** - It's not right.

**SIMON** - I'm not right. I don't belong here. That's the truth. I'm an intruder. But I won't let these machines be turned over to authorities who won't understand them. They would destroy them just trying to figure them out.

**ULI** - You could be right. And maybe you don't care because this is not your country. But it is mine. Good day, Herr Meier.

*Uli exits*

**MAX** - I had been reckless, speaking so openly about my purpose. I wanted to make more recordings, but I could also sense a growing danger. Uli wouldn't remain silent much longer. That night, I threaded up the tape I had made of the Dobos record. Celestially, it was the wrong time, but I thought I'd better attempt a return trip.

*Simon arranges the tape machine and speakers, and the small tone generator. He plays the Dobos tape. The critical moment arrives, and there is some minor disturbance, but no transportation results. He shuts off the tone generator.*

**MAX** - No luck. I couldn't reproduce the effect, not that night. I managed to shake the floor a bit, that was all.

*As the melody continues, Bach enters the room.*

**BACH** - My Partita Number 2, D minor.

**SIMON** - Herr Bach.

**BACH** - And this is the object that has so agitated Herr Falkenrath.

**SIMON** - He told you.

**BACH** - Oh yes. May I?

**SIMON** - Of course.

*Bach examines the machine as it continues to play*

**BACH** - Your science is astonishing. So these are captured sounds. If I may ask, who is this playing?

**SIMON** - Her name is Irena Dobos.

**BACH** - Hungarian. I can hear it in her phrasing. Like it's a folk song. Too emotional. She needs greater precision.

**SIMON** - I've heard critics say that they find her too technical, too dry.

**BACH** - No, no. This is sentimental. Is she well known?

**SIMON** - Not yet.

**BACH** - I suppose there is a public who will embrace such theatrics. You know what they say. If the people cheer, it wasn't played correctly.

*Enter Katarina*

**KATARINA** - Oh! Oh, Herr Meier, that is magical!

**SIMON** - Katarina.

**KATARINA** - I love the Chaconne. It makes me think of mother. I haven't heard this played in a long time.

**BACH** - Herr Meier, I was composing this piece when my first wife took ill. God was merciful and she did not suffer for long. But for me, this piece has always seemed a kind of memorial to her. As such, I confess it brings sadness in the hearing.

*Simon turns off the music*

**BACH** - I understand your wish to keep this secret. Some might claim you had devils enslaved in that machine.

**SIMON** - Not at all. It's just vibrations captured and amplified. In a way, it's not much more than a sophisticated music box.

**BACH** - If it won't trouble you, I would hear a bit of the cantata you captured last week.

**SIMON** - *(changing reels)* All right. I was pleased with the result of that recording. One moment.

*Once the new reel is set, he switches it on. The Magnificat plays.*

**KATARINA** - It's fantastic. If I closed my eyes, I might think I was standing in the sanctuary.

**BACH** - Young master Grauenstadt must mind his intonation. His pitch tends to go sharp if he's not careful. Very well, that's enough. *(Simon turns off the tape machine)*

**SIMON** - I hope you aren't angry, Herr Bach.

**BACH** - Angry, no. But as to this astonishing invention, I don't approve.

**KATARINA** - You don't?

**BACH** - Let's say you commit to your machine all of the greatest musicians, the works of every major composer. Then what? Why should I continue to practice and perfect my art when I can just as easily activate this contraption. It will encourage idleness, and promote an attitude of leisure and laziness. If you want my honest prophecy, Herr Meier, I believe this clever toy will kill the art. I thank you for allowing me access to your experiment, and now, I beg you to remove it from my school. Let it never cross my attention again.

**KATARINA** - Papa ...

**BACH** - Good night, Herr Meier.

**SIMON** - Thank you, Herr Bach. Good night.

*Bach and Katarina exit. Uli enters and begins moving items out of the cabinet. Once finished, he exits.*

# 1-I: A Small Flat in Leipzig

*The DL corner of the stage has become Simon's new home, a tiny workshop. Simon sets up art supplies, paint brushes and canvases. He also places two solar collectors on the farthest end of the space, near a window so that they can recharge. The tape machine rests beneath it.*

**MAX** - As quickly as that, my access to St. Thomas came to an end. Uli was good enough to help me find cheap lodging. He helped me to move everything safely, and secretly. I was truly on my own in that world. I had to make some kind of living. And what marketable skill did I have? Art. I turned my small flat into a workshop. Landscapes and still lifes. Over time, I built up a clientele. My style was loose and simple. It appealed to the children of noblemen and wealthy patrons. And because I wanted to stay in his good graces, I made art for the youngest children of Herr Bach.

*Enter Katarina. She picks up a small canvas with an elephant brightly painted in gaudy colors. She laughs when she sees it.*

**KATARINA** - Regina will love it. These colors are ...

**SIMON** - Garish and painful to look at.

**KATARINA** - Which is exactly what she likes.

**SIMON** - She was very specific about the proper coloring for an elephant. Now, I'll wrap this, but you've got to be careful with it.

*He wraps the painting in cloth and string*

**KATARINA** - I wish you'd let us give you something for it.

**SIMON** - It's my pleasure. I'll always owe your family a debt of gratitude.

**KATARINA** - Herr Meier, I want to ask you something. I hope you won't be alarmed. It's about that machine of yours.

**SIMON** - The one I'm not to speak of again.

**KATARINA** - Yes. It's been on my mind ever since I heard it.

**SIMON** - I hope it hasn't troubled you, or your father.

**KATARINA** - He's never talked about it. But yes, it troubles me.

**SIMON** - I'm sorry, Fraulein. I never meant for anyone to know about it.

**KATARINA** - Can you tell me how it works?

**SIMON** - Well ... yes, I suppose I could.

**KATARINA** - There's no real reason why. I'm often curious about things. I seldom have a chance to learn firsthand.

**SIMON** - Curiosity is a good thing. When I was a child, I used to take things apart to see how they worked. In five minutes, I could take apart a clock, a watch, a radio.

**KATARINA** - A radio?

**SIMON** - Ah. Never mind that. It's a piece of technical equipment. My father was an engineer. I took after him.

**KATARINA** - So, what does a radio do?

**SIMON** - Let's start with the recording machine.

**KATARINA** - I know that an organ can imitate the sound of a flute, or trumpet. But I have never heard anything sound so life-like. An entire orchestra and choir, and the voice of young Grauenstadt.

**SIMON** - The mystery isn't so hard to solve. Every sound is nothing more than pulses of air, a wave. Here, I can show you.

*Lights lower and Max narrates from spot*

**MAX** - Katarina was an excellent student. And my explanations may have been simplified, but they represented knowledge that nobody else on Earth at that time could have shared with her.

*Lights back up. Simon plugs headphones into the tape drive*

**SIMON** - We don't even have to amplify the sound. You can hear it through these.

*He tries them on first, adjusts the volume, then helps to place them over Katarina's ears.*

**SIMON** - This is the sound of your father rehearsing a fugue on the church organ.

**KATARINA** - And this device carries the sound to the machine.

**SIMON** - The microphone. Right. There's a metal coil inside that vibrates in response to pulses in the air. That vibration becomes a signal. The signal travels along this cable and vibrates the membranes inside of the speaker. Or inside of those headphones.

**KATARINA** - Headphones.

**SIMON** - Right. There's nothing spooky about it.

**KATARINA** - So, if I talk into this microphone ...

**SIMON** - Yes, I can record you. Here. Let me wind this past the music. *(He does so)* Now, when I turn this knob and press this button, the reels will turn, and you can say whatever you like into the microphone.

**KATARINA** - Wait! What should I say?

**SIMON** - Anything. Just say your name. *(He starts the recording)* Go ahead.

**KATARINA** - My name is Katarina Dorothea Bach.

*He stops, rewinds and plays it back "My name is Katarina Dorothea Bach." Katarina lets out a quick yelp, then laughs.*

**KATARINA** - Is that what my voice sounds like?

**SIMON** - Yes.

**KATARINA** - But it can't be!

**SIMON** - It's true. Almost everybody hates the sound of their own voice the first time they hear it.

**KATARINA** - Almost everybody? Who else even knows about this?

**SIMON** - Here in Leipzig, nobody but you, your father, and Uli. I hope.

**KATARINA** - But where you live?

**SIMON** - It's commonplace. In fact, this equipment is obsolete.

**KATARINA** - But how is that possible? Everyone in the colonies has this?

**SIMON** - Well no, not now.

**KATARINA** - But they all know about it.

**SIMON** - Not yet.

**KATARINA** - You aren't making any sense.

**SIMON** - You're right. I'm sorry. I forget where I am sometimes. I'd better put this away.

**KATARINA** - Please wait. I'm still very curious. What are these?

**SIMON** - Batteries. They store electrical power. The machine can't run without them.

**KATARINA** - What kind of power?

**SIMON** - Electricity. I shouldn't be telling you this.

**KATARINA** - *(Sitting on the large chair, leaning forward curiously)* I've heard of electricity. Lightning ...

**SIMON** - Yes, well this device can convert the heat from the sunlight.

**KATARINA** - How?

**SIMON** - Even I don't know everything.

**KATARINA** - Show me.

**SIMON** - I can't.

**KATARINA** - Why not? I know about your sound machine. I want to know about electricity.

**SIMON** - This was a mistake, Fraulein. It was wrong for me to be so candid.

**KATARINA** - *(standing)* I apologize, Herr Meier. I didn't mean to pry.

**SIMON** - Don't mention it.

**KATARINA** - But that's not really true, is it. I clearly meant to pry.

**SIMON** - And I clearly enjoyed talking about it.

**KATARINA** - I'll never speak of it again. Good day, Herr Meier.

*She picks up the package with the elephant painting and begins to leave.*

**SIMON** - Electricity is a property of all physical matter.

**KATARINA** - *(turning back to him)* Yes?

**SIMON** - Break down the material world into its smallest components, and they are made up of electric impulses. Positive and negative.

*Katarina sets the package down and stands very close, facing him*

**KATARINA** - So, you and I are electric.

**SIMON** - Everything is.

**KATARINA** - Then it's the divine spark.

*They share a brief kiss*

**SIMON** - Yes. Divine.

*They kiss again, passionately, as lights fade.*

 END ACT ONE

# Act Two

*During Intermission, the largest chair has been placed in front of the rest of the tiny flat. The chair is draped in bedclothes, and a few ornate pillows. The visual suggestion is that this is a bed, rumpled and disheveled by an amorous tryst. Simon and Katarina take their place in the darkness before the second act begins. (They may play the scene with both on the chair, or with both on the floor, comfortably intimate.)*

# 2-A: The Flat in Leipzig



**MAX** - I fell in love with Katarina over the course of a single conversation. Prior to that, I hadn't paid much attention to her. Unfairly, I had judged her as prim, because she was on the school staff, because she was a little older than I. But that day, her curiosity showed me someone so alive and engaged.

We spent as many afternoons together as we could. And yes. I told her everything. Well, almost everything. There are some secrets I've kept from everyone, Simon. I won't keep them from you.

*Lights up on chair. Simon and Katarina are in an intimate spooning embrace.*

**KATARINA** - It makes no sense.

**SIMON** - I know it doesn't. And I can't expect you to believe me.

**KATARINA** - But I do. Sometimes I do.

**SIMON** - Really?

**KATARINA** - When I'm here with you. It's the only explanation. A man from tomorrow who can capture sunlight and turn it into music. It's when I leave that my mind tells me it's impossible.

**SIMON** - Do you know what I'd like to do? I want to record your voice singing.

**KATARINA** - I haven't sung for years.

**SIMON** - But you used to.

**KATARINA** - I did. Mostly to teach the children. When my mother was alive, I sang with her all the time. Father even told me I was 'not terrible.' That's high praise.

**SIMON** - Did you sing publicly?

**KATARINA** - Oh, no. We sang at home, for guests, for one another. I don't think Papa would approve of a daughter who seeks an audience.

**SIMON** - Why not? Faustina and Cuzzoni have become wealthy and famous at the opera.

**KATARINA** - Ha! My father would not approve. He thinks opera is just noise and rude spectacle.

**SIMON** - It is! So we should go.

**KATARINA** - What?

**SIMON** - We should go to the opera. Have you ever been?

**KATARINA** - Well, no I haven't.

**SIMON** - Then let me accompany you.

**KATARINA** - Publicly? I'd be recognized. 72

**SIMON** - It doesn't have to be Leipzig. I'll take you to Prague.

**KATARINA** - You're going to smuggle me away to Bohemia?

**SIMON** - Yes, and we won't stop there. I'll take you to Luxembourg, Vienna ... hell, I can take you to Philadelphia.

**KATARINA** - Max! It's the kind of thing I dream about.

**SIMON** - Then we should do it.

**KATARINA** - No. My way is set. I will be Frau Falkenrath. It's posted, signed and sealed.

**SIMON** - Escape it.

**KATARINA** - This is my escape, Max. But it can't last forever. As long as I am in Leipzig, there is only one way for things to go.

**SIMON** - Then don't stay in Leipzig.

**KATARINA** - My family is here. My father, my brothers and sisters. They are my life, Max. They always will be.

**SIMON** - Good. But why Uli Falkenrath, if you don't love him?

**KATARINA** - Because it's been decided.

**SIMON** - Not by you. If you lived in my time ...

**KATARINA** - But I don't. Max, I will not entertain this fantasy. *She stands and readies herself to leave*

**SIMON** - Every time you leave, I'm afraid it will be the last time. *(no reply)* This time, it is.

**KATARINA** - I'm sorry, Max. This has been glorious, and wrong.

**SIMON** - Not wrong, Katarina. We are free people, or should be.

*Katarina sits in the small wooden chair*

**KATARINA** - My world isn't about freedom. It's about duty. Father arranged for me to take up the post at the school when I was twenty-three. Thirteen years ago. He feared I would never find a husband, but he told me that through work, I would find useful purpose for my life.

**SIMON** - And did you?

**KATARINA** - Yes, often. At least, once Herr Kromner was gone.

**SIMON** - Who is he?

**KATARINA** - He was supervisor when I began. I disliked him the first time he summoned me to his office. He was one of those hateful men who has a little bit of power. His punishments were harsh and arbitrary. He said it was right that the students fear him. They certainly hated him.

I once dared to speak up for a boy, the youngest in the school. He was accused for things the older boys had done. I tried to appeal to Herr Kromner. I asked him to stop punishing the boy unjustly. Herr Kromner took it as defiance. He began making up lies about me. He told my family that I was a thief, that I was too familiar with the boys, that I incited them to rebellious behavior. He insisted that I spend time with him for what he called corrective counseling.

Perhaps you can guess where this story leads. He coerced me into his bed. He made it clear that if I spoke, it would mean injury or death.

This terrible arrangement didn't last for long. I became pregnant. No one ever speaks about it, but everyone knows. It's the secret scandal of my life. Herr Kromner was removed from his post. He found employment somewhere else. No injury to his reputation. As for me, the child died in my womb. I almost died myself, on the surgeon's table.

I will never have children of my own. Papa likes to pretend that I might. He knows better. But he doesn't like to accept it.

My family is everything, Max. We are imperfect, and we have had our share of grief. But we have a bond of trust. Uli has been accepted into this trust. He knows the facts of my life, and he respects me. Maybe he even loves me.

You, Max, you have been a strange and wonderful dream. I'm not even sure that you're real, but I know I lack the imagination to have invented you. This time with you has brought me happiness I didn't think possible. I used you as my escape. It was selfish of me to indulge in it. You don't belong here. I don't belong next to you. But I will always remember. Goodbye, Max.

*She exits. Light transition to Simon and Max in the present.*

# 2-B: A Street at Night

**MAX** - And that was the end of it. I didn't plead, I didn't pursue her. She was right. I didn't belong there.

**SIMON** - Did you ever see her again?

**MAX** - Only once, years later.

**SIMON** - So let me guess where this is going. Your love for her was the real deal, but my love for Heather isn't.

**MAX** - That's not where I'm going. But yes, Katarina certainly taught me something about love. Not for the time she spent with me. The love she had for everyone who shared her life. The sick she cared for and the dying she comforted. I was never going to be a true part of that. But I do think I learned something by example. Accept the gift when it's given to you. And don't try to wrestle it back if it's withdrawn.

**SIMON** - Well, news flash. The gift has never been offered to me.

**MAX** - And likely never will be. Not as long as you act like Simon the Sniveler.

**SIMON** - At least I'm not Max the Moralist. I hope I'm never this sanctimonious.

**MAX** - I hope you're never anything like me! You're still 22. But when you're 24, you must be very careful, Simon Lexner. Do not become what I am.

**SIMON** - And what is that?

**MAX** - A murderer.

*Lights change. Sound of pounding on a door. In darkness, Simon exits.*

**ULI** - *(offstage)* Max Meier! Max Meier, open this door! *(pounds again)* Herr Meier!

**MAX** - There's not much more to tell. Herr Falkenrath came pounding at my door late one evening, about a month after my final tryst with Katarina. I knew better than to let him in. Instead, I did the brave thing and crept out the window at the back of my flat. But he found me.

*Enter Simon. Uli runs to him and begins punching him. Simon fights back at first, then tears himself away.*

**SIMON** - Stop! Herr Falkenrath, that's enough. I'm not very strong.

**ULI** - You are a shit. You're a monster, and probably a spy.

**SIMON** - I'm not a spy.

*Uli hits him a strong blow. Simon collapses.*

**ULI** - You should have known I'd have someone keeping watch on you. With the kind of secrets you keep, you will always have someone watching.

**SIMON** - I'm not a threat to anyone.

**ULI** - You're a threat to Herr Bach.

**SIMON** - What do you mean?

**ULI** - I mean that your iniquity has been exposed. I have called out your affair with Katarina. She has been sent away in shame and disgrace.

*Simon jumps up at Uli and wrestles him to the ground.*

**SIMON** - Where is she?

**ULI** - Gone! You won't see her again!

*Simon hits Uli, they scuffle some more, then tire. The two remain on the ground, exhausted from the fight.*

**SIMON** - And you. Will you go to her now? Will you marry her?

**ULI** - I have no place in my life for such a woman.

**SIMON** - She trusted you. She said you were understanding.

**ULI** - Until this betrayal, I was. Now that I know the truth, I've exposed her, Herr Meier. I have exposed you as well. The burgomaster is in your home right now. Your unholy implements are being confiscated. You will be arrested. If you are inclined to run, you had best go now, before I shout for help.

*Simon gets to his feet and exits. Uli follows after*

**MAX** - I did run. And he did shout.

**ULI** - *(running offstage)* Capture him! Arrest him!

**MAX** - I just managed to get out of the city gates. Every one of my belongings was collected from that room and locked away.

# 2-C: The Shop (2nd Interlude)

*Present-day Simon enters during the following*

**MAX** - I hid in the forests and hiked out of sight of the road. I made my way to Mittelsachsen and hid for a while in Dresden. I found a cheap place to bide my time in Altenburg. I hired on as a custodian at an inn. I cleaned up after drunken travelers. I kept an eye on men who came to challenge the local card sharks. Eventually, I learned how to swindle travelers at the game of Skat. I became a low-level crook. It kept me alive. I spent five years in exile at that grimy pit of an inn.

**SIMON** - When did you kill Uli?

**MAX** - I didn't.

**SIMON** - You said you're a murderer.

**MAX** - And I am. But I didn't kill Herr Falkenrath. He perished on his own, sometime in 1763, according to his gravestone.

**SIMON** - Who did you kill?

**MAX** - If I tell you, I want you to promise me you'll stay and hear the end of my story. It's going to upset you.

**SIMON** - What do you mean?

**MAX** - I didn't kill anyone in the 18th century, Simon. I killed in the 21st. Before the leap. Just before I returned to Leipzig, I killed in Pennsylvania. It's why I changed my name. Simon Lexner made the leap from jealous asshole to cold-blooded killer. Max Meier is the name he chose to hide behind.

**SIMON** - Heather?

**MAX** - No. I didn't kill Heather. Now listen carefully. This could be your future, though I sure as hell hope it won't be. I've told you how I intruded on the two of them when I went back to the States. In truth, I was an emotional bully. I tried to play Heather and David off against one another. I tried to disrupt their happiness.

They began avoiding me, and who could blame them. They must have sensed the danger. They sure as hell un-friended me.

On March 3rd, 2016, I found out they were going to the cabin owned by David's uncle. The one up by Lake Harmony. You've been there. They went to spend a snowbound weekend away from me. I got a bus ride and followed them.

That night, I spied on them through the windows of the cabin. I looked on as they shared a bed. Yes Simon, it's just as sick as you fear. Later, while Heather slept, David saw me through the window. He came out after me. We got into a fight.

I strangled him. It wasn't self-defense. He was never very strong. I overpowered him. I knocked him unconscious. And while he was out, I put my hands around his throat and ended his life.

Now you know. When I was 24, I took a life, fled my home country and became another person.

*Simon doesn't speak, but looks at Max in disbelief.*

I disconnected. I told myself that the Dobos project was too important. I was advancing science. I invented a good man called Max, and I buried a violent coward called Simon. It was a good disguise. I wasn't found out until September. I would have been captured and extradited, except that I had a way out that nobody could follow me through. And just in time, I took it.

On the afternoon of Thursday, September 16, on the Autumn equinox, I left the 21st century. It was the culmination of David's work. I tried to pretend it somehow made up for my own crime. *(After a silence)* I hope you're angry. I hope you're at least shocked.

**SIMON** - I wish you hadn't escaped. I wish you had just died.

**MAX** - If I had, would you even be here?

**SIMON** - Does it matter?

**MAX** - I think it does.

**SIMON** - I don't want to know anything more about you.

**MAX** - That's fine. You've heard the worst of it. The rest is up to you.

**SIMON** - David is alive.

**MAX** - Yes. He is. Now, I don't know if that's true in every possible universe. It could be he's alive in this stream, but somewhere else, there's a world where he is dead and I'm his killer. I'll never know. But in this world, David lives. And he can keep on living.

You still have the gift of innocence. I don't. Even knowing he is alive here, I will always have the memory. I will always know how it felt, how much force it took to squeeze the life out of him. I'll remember the way he opened his eyes at the last moment, just in time for my face to be the last thing he saw. Maybe I've managed a cosmic reset, and really truly fixed things. Maybe I haven't. But I get to play that scene over and over in my mind. There's a good chance it'll be the last thing I think of when I die.

Are you all right?

**SIMON** - No.

**MAX** - You should be.

**SIMON** - I can't be. I've already had those kind of thoughts. You know that. The first time I even suspected, I had violent thoughts.

**MAX** - And now you can let them go. You can grow out of them.

*Lights fade out except on Max as he continues. Simon exits in the darkness.*

# 2-D: A Room at St. Thomas School

**MAX** - I may as well finish my story. After five years in Altenburg, I returned to Leipzig for a festival. It was 1750, and Carl Phillip Emmanuel Bach was conducting the first public performance of his father's B Minor Mass. I couldn't resist going, just to hear it for myself. I'm sure you can appreciate that.

*B minor Mass begins to play*

My plan was to attend anonymously, and then slink away as soon as it was over. But I was seen and recognized. An official from the St. Thomas School found me. He asked me to accompany him back to the school. He assured me that Herr Bach would want to speak to me.

*Music fades as Bach appears, wearing dark spectacles over his eyes. He seems weak as he takes a seat.*

These were the last weeks of his life. After an operation on his eyes, he was almost completely blind. He would soon undergo a second surgery, and I knew he would die shortly after that.

**BACH** - Please come in, Herr Meier.

*Simon enters cautiously*

**SIMON** - Herr Bach.

**BACH** - In these last several years, I had nearly forgotten about you. I imagined you might have left the country.

**SIMON** - I probably should have. I've grieved you, Herr Bach. And I can't begin to apologize ...

**BACH** - Then don't. Please. Not now, Herr Meier. I want to tell you what has happened since you disappeared.

**SIMON** - Please.

**BACH** - A committee of military officers were called together to examine your strange machines. I was asked to give an account of everything I knew about them.

**SIMON** - Do they still have them?

**BACH** - I regret to say every piece of your equipment was dismantled, or in some cases simply smashed apart. The committee seemed to think your machines were not the product of human industry. They were called infernal.

**SIMON** - Is there anyone I could talk to?

**BACH** - I wouldn't advise it, young man. I have no joy in saying so, but you are strange and unsettling. Not without charm, and possessing rare knowledge. But the men who run this city will be far less tolerant than I have been.

**SIMON** - Of course.

**BACH** - Katarina has only recently returned from a long stay in Hamburg. We have spoken about the brief time the two of you shared. I cannot condone what went on, but I don't deny that for her, the memory is pleasant and sustaining. *(Bach hesitates for a beat)* She tells me you are from another time, Herr Meier. You come from the Philadelphia of a distant tomorrow. Is this true?

**SIMON** - Yes, Herr Bach.

**BACH** - So, you really did hear my concerti played in Philadelphia, but it hasn't happened yet. Is this right?

**SIMON** - Yes. It will happen more than two-hundred and fifty years from now.

**BACH** - So my music will survive that long.

**SIMON** - Forever. You're on the short list of the greatest composers of all time, along with Mozart and Beethoven.

**BACH** - I don't know them.

**SIMON** - They're not here yet.

**BACH** - Why did you do it? If my music is still played so frequently in your own time, why take such risks to come here?

**SIMON** - I wanted to hear it at the source. I wanted to witness it and capture it. I wanted to have a recording so precious that it would be impossible to fix a price to it.

**BACH** - I should be flattered. But my music is not to be caught and contained. It is to be performed. It exists to bring the light of God to those persons attending it. But I forget, you have no God.

**SIMON** - No. I don't think any of us do. I think we only have each other. And even if your music doesn't bring me closer to God, it gives me peace. It brings me reassurance and strength. It makes me want to be better than the criminal that I am.

**BACH** - No more, Herr Meier. I am not your confessor, and I will not be the object of your devotion. Stay here as our guest. Tomorrow morning, Katarina will arrive, and will be glad to see you.

*Bach stands and wavers.*

**SIMON** - I'll help you, Herr Bach.

*Simon goes takes his arm as guidance as the nearly sightless Bach slowly makes his exit.*

**BACH** - Fine. *(They take a few steps, then stop)* One last question. Is it common for men of the future to invade the past?

**SIMON** - I don't know. I'm not aware of anyone else who has done it.

**BACH** - Was Practice Hall 12 the gate through which you passed?

**SIMON** - Yes.

**BACH** - It's always been a strange place. Uneasy. It is disturbing, but intriguing. Much like you. I hope that someday you will find safe passage back to where you belong. And now, I intend never to think about the matter again. Good rest, Herr Meier.

*Bach takes leave of him*

**MAX** - He was right. This room has always been an anomaly. The Dobos effect is only the most obvious manifestation. This place intensifies everything. Music. Feelings. Regrets.

*Enter Katarina*

**KATARINA** - Max?

*Katarina runs to Max and embraces him*

**KATARINA** - I was sure I would never see you again.

**SIMON** - Katarina. I'm ashamed to be seen. In these last five years, I've only fallen. I live a dishonest life.

**KATARINA** - And that is my fault. My actions made you vulnerable. I trusted in Uli, and he rejoiced in the destruction of your life's work. All of your machines are gone, Max.

**SIMON** - I know. I should never have come here. I disrupted your life. Your father's life.

**KATARINA** - If you hadn't, I would be married to Uli now. And I no longer think that would have been a good thing. He was a better man than Herr Kromner. But in the end, he revealed his own cruelty. We did not belong together.

**SIMON** - You said that about me too.

**KATARINA** - Maybe people shouldn't belong to each other. Maybe they should just celebrate whatever time they have.

**SIMON** - I wish we'd had more.

**KATARINA** - What we had was perfect. I would ask for no less. (Simon moves to embrace her. She stops him) And no more. I have something to give you.

*She opens the cabinet. Inside are reels of tape.*

**KATARINA** - These escaped Uli's notice.

*Simon picks up and looks at the tape reels*

**SIMON** - You saved the recordings.

**KATARINA** - They've been hidden away for five years. Is there anything you can do with them?

**SIMON** - No. But if they survive, they will be the greatest cultural treasure of all time. *(A thought occurs)* Oh! Wait!

*Simon goes to the cabinet and opens one of the small drawers. He removes a can of coffee.*

**SIMON** - This entire drawer. It was never emptied.

**KATARINA** - What is it?

**SIMON** - Coffee of the future. Here. Try it. They don't spoil.

*He hands it to Katarina and retrieves another. He opens and drinks. Katarina follows suit.*

**SIMON** - It's better when it's cold.

**KATARINA** - It's so sweet.

**SIMON** - And if the coffee is still here ...

*He opens the second drawer and reaches into it, pulling out a wrapped bundle. He unravels it to reveal a Walkman cassette recorder.*

**SIMON** - To think I almost didn't pack this.

*He presses the play button. No movement. He shakes the cloth, and a pack of batteries falls out.*

**SIMON** - And there we are.

**KATARINA** - What is it?

**SIMON** - A second chance. Maybe.

**KATARINA** - For you to get back?

**SIMON** - I hope so. But there's something else I can do now. Something important.

**KATARINA** - What is it?

**SIMON** - *(putting in the batteries)* This is a recorder. It does everything the larger machine did, just not as well. Katarina, I want you to sing. I want to record your voice.

**KATARINA** - What, now?

**SIMON** - Will there be any other time?

**KATARINA** - No.

**SIMON** - Then, please.

**KATARINA** - I'm not rehearsed. I'm not ready to ...

**SIMON** - It doesn't matter, Katarina. Please. It doesn't have to be pure or perfect. It just has to be you. Here, in this room.

*Katarina looks hesitant, but approaches the small recorder and opens her mouth to sing. The lights fade out.*

# 2-F: The Shop

*Spotlight on Max. The sound of Katarina's voice is heard for the next few moments.*

**MAX** - She sang, and I recorded it onto a Maxell cassette tape. She chose one of her father's most profound songs. Komm Susser Tod.

*The sound of singing continues: "Komm Susser Tod, Komm Heilig Ru,"*

"Come Sweet Death, Come Blessed Rest, Lead Me To Peace, For This World Has Made Me Weary." No accompaniment. Just her own priceless voice. And in the middle of the song, the room sounded with sympathetic harmonic vibration. I captured it on tape.

An hour later, I was escorted out to the city gate. It was many years before I was able to return to this room.

Just as I knew must happen, Herr Bach died on the morning of July 28 1750. Even knowing in advance, I grieved.

In all, I spent four decades in the past. I survived periods of epidemic and war. I even made a voyage to America. I wanted to be sure I was in Philadelphia when the Declaration was signed. You see, I am a patriotic expat after all.

On September 22nd, 1784, I snuck back into this room, an old man. Outside, there was an electrical storm. I don't know if that helped me or not. I put the last of my batteries into that cassette player, and hooked it to a primitive set of conical speakers I had made myself. I packed the cabinet with items that at the time would have seemed quite ordinary, but that in the 21st century became priceless antiques. At midnight, I played the only recording I had on cassette, Katarina singing. And it worked. I was back. I landed in 2012, sick, suffering and 62 years old.

*The lights come up gradually, revealing the present day Simon listening to the end of Max's story.*

My little hoard of treasures gave me the money I needed to open my unique little shop. And now here we are.

**SIMON** - Here we are.

**MAX** - I promised you that if you would listen to my story, I would reward you with the rarest of records. *(He presents a 7" vinyl single)* This was a limited pressing. Just one. A 7 inch single. 45 rpm. Nothing on Side B. On Side A, the daughter of Johann Sebastian Bach singing Komm Susser Tod. Mastered from the analog cassette, which is broken and unplayable. Take it home with you. It's divine music, Simon. Born of sorrow and suffering, transformed into the only glory I've ever known.

**SIMON** - Then you should have it.

**MAX** - I do. In here. Locked in my memory with perfect fidelity. *(He hands the record to Simon.)*

**SIMON** - What happens now? I mean, everything has changed.

**MAX** - I hope so. I really hope so.

**SIMON** - But what should I do?

**MAX** - It's up to you. You have new knowledge of yourself. And in me, you have a role model whose example you must shun.

*Simon looks at the record.*

**SIMON** - May I play it now?

**MAX** - Here?

**SIMON** - Yes. Please.

*Max considers*

**MAX** - All right.

**SIMON** - Alone. I'd like to hear her voice without ...

**MAX** - Without my endless yapping? I'll tell you what. I'm going to go into my kitchen and eat something. You listen. If you'd like to stay and talk about it, that's fine. If you'd rather take your things and go back to the school, I'll understand. There's nothing more for me to tell you anyway.

**SIMON** - Thank you.

**MAX** - Simon, it's too early for me to ask. But have I gotten through? Can you put away your jealousy? *(after a pause)* Right. Too early to ask. *(He exits to the kitchen)*

*Simon waits until Max is gone. He puts the 7 inch record down on a table and pulls out the original Irena Dobos record instead. He places it on the turntable, puts down the needle partway through. The Chaconne begins to play. He turns the dial on the harmonic generator. The room begins to rumble.*

**MAX** - *(appearing at kitchen doorway)* Simon! Wait! *(The noise grows louder and the lights begin to flicker)* Simon!

*Max ducks back through door. A loud rumble and the sound of breaking glass, then darkness. When the light returns. Simon is gone. Smoke rises from the turntable. Max enters and picks up the Dobos record. It has melted. He opens the cabinet. It's empty.*

**MAX** - Exactly what I would have done.

*He sees Simon's cell phone nearby. He picks it up.*

# 2-G: The Shop, Two Years Later

*Transition – Max changes into a different coat, and places a sign on the front of the cabinet. It reads:*

*SUMMER 2016*

*FINAL CLEARANCE SALE*

*Sommer 2016 Endgültige Spiel Verkauf*

*Max begins to gather and put things away. After a few moments, he hears a ringtone. He picks up Simon's cell phone and looks at it.*

**MAX** - I'll be damned.

*He reads, then begins texting.*

**MAX** - "Good to hear from you. Hope you are both well. Simon"

*He sends the text and puts down the phone. In another few moments, Heather enters the store.*

**MAX** - Ah. May I help you?

**HEATHER** - Hi. Max, right?

**MAX** - Yes. And you're Heather Grenado.

**HEATHER** - That's right.

**MAX** - I was hoping you might stop by someday. Simon has told me a lot about you.

**HEATHER** - Is he here? I just sent him a text. *(Looks at her phone)* Oh. He answered.

**MAX** - He's traveling. I don't see him here much these days.

**HEATHER** - I was hoping I might find him. My fiancé and I are here for a couple of days, and I thought he might ...

**MAX** - I remember the day you came in here with him. It was last year?

**HEATHER** - Two years ago. It was actually the last time I saw him in person.

**MAX** - Oh.

**HEATHER** - I'm sorry, but ...

**MAX** - There's something about me. Yes, I know. Maybe Simon never told you. I'm his uncle Max. There's some family resemblance.

**HEATHER** - I'll say. It's kind of spooky.

**MAX** - So he never mentioned it?

**HEATHER** - No. Well, if you talk to him, please tell him I came by. I'd like to get in touch if it's okay with him.

**MAX** - I'll tell him.

**HEATHER** - We're getting married in March. I don't know if he'd want to come.

**MAX** - I guess you're aware, he was pretty taken with you. HEATHER - Yeah. David and I, we really felt terrible about it.

**MAX** - I wouldn't worry. Simon is out seeing new worlds. But send him a picture. He'll like that.

**HEATHER** - I appreciate it. *(She notices the sign)* So, you're going out of business?

**MAX** - Retiring. I'll be leaving Leipzig soon.

**HEATHER** - Too bad. It's a really cool store.

**MAX** - Thank you.

**HEATHER** - Well, bye.

**MAX** - Hold on. There's something here I think you should have. (*He retrieves the butterfly painting.*) Simon was going to give this to you in person when he had a chance. He made it.

**HEATHER** - I remember this. Wait, he made it?

**SIMON** - It was meant to be a surprise.

*Heather gives Max a long look, then turns her attention to the painting. Then she looks back at Max, intently, focused on his face.*

**HEATHER** - *(Beginning to see who Max really is)* Of course. I should have known.

*She steps away, holding the picture.*

**HEATHER** - *(fighting off her realization)* Thank you. I ... I wish you the best of luck.

*She turns and leaves quickly.*

**MAX** - *(quietly)* Goodbye

*Simon begins clearing items out of one of the cabinet drawers. He looks surprised to find a scroll, bound with a ribbon, coated with the dust of age.*

**MAX** - Now what? I don't remember you being in here before.

*He opens it and begins to read.*

**MAX** - "Dear Max." What in the ...

*He looks at the bottom of the rolled paper*

**MAX** - From Simon. *(He sits down before continuing to read)* "Dear Max, I have placed this letter into the cabinet in Practice Hall 12 in hopes that it might find you. If this has fallen into other hands, it will make little sense."

*Simon appears nearby, dimly lit. He remains mostly in shadow as he speaks the next passage of the letter.*

**SIMON** - I thought you might like to know that I made it to Leipzig. I arrived with no money, no belongings. I made an impulsive decision, and as you know, I lack the means to attempt a return trip. I am here for life.

I did it to escape myself. I ran to avoid facing my own jealousy. I ran so that I would never have to learn firsthand how much worse it could get.

I work for the St. Thomas School, and I have now for many years. I was well established by the time Herr Bach and his family moved in.

For you see, unlike you, I arrived in 1712, long before Herr Bach became Cantor. If you still think of me as the young man who disappeared from your shop, you should know that I am now eighty-four years old ...

**MAX** - Eighty-four ...

**SIMON** - I worked alongside Katarina. We enjoyed a companionable friendship. But by then, I was considerably older, nothing like the young stranger Max who might have stolen her heart in some other shadow world. There is no Max here, and never was. I remain Simon Lexner to this day.

*Simon recedes further into shadow.*

**MAX** - (reading) "I write this to you in the year 1774. Katarina was laid to rest just days ago. I imagine you still think of her often. I want to tell you something that may bring comfort. Because I arrived so early, and because I pursued this post at the school, nobody else has held the position. Not Uli Falkenrath, and more importantly, not Herr Kromner. They have never been a part of Katarina's life. I trust your heart will be glad to consider what this means.

You have been given a world in which David Caro lives. I have a world in which Katarina was never treated with cruelty. My intrusion into this world, by glad fortune, has spared her some measure of suffering.

*Max stops reading, stunned by the implications of what he has read. He sets the letter down and takes an almost prayerful moment to let it sink in. As the final words are read, Max rises and goes to the turntable.*

**SIMON** - *(heard but unseen)* Maybe these worlds are not real. Maybe they are just analog. Perhaps they are built on nothing more than threads of divine sound, fragile vibrations suspended in the unfathomable.

*Max places the 7-inch single on the turntable. There is the sound of the needle drop, then the voice of Katarina begins to sing 'Komm Susser Tod.' There is a slight swell of harmonic tones and a dimming of light. Suddenly, Katarina is present in the room, an apparition in faint blue light. The audio of the recording gives way to the sound of her actual voice, singing live. Max kneels before her and looks up in admiration.*

**KATARINA** - *(singing)*

Komm, süßer Tod, komm, selge Ruh/ Im Himmel ist es besser, da alle Lust viel größer/ drum bin ich jederzeit, schon zum Valet bereit/ ich schließ die Augen, Komm, selge Ruh!

END

# Production Notes

The original production of Analog took place in a small warehouse theater, with about 300 seats. This proved to be the right size of venue, not so big as to overwhelm, not so small as to restrict what we could achieve. Achieving a distinction between present day and past was largely a matter of lighting, costuming, and context.

Essentially, we created the record store onstage, and maintained the ambiance that the audience was visiting an eclectic shop in an old building. When the past takes over the narrative, much of the setting was draped or covered, and we spot-lit small sections of Max's store for the interludes back at the shop in the 21st century. Productions are encouraged to represent both present and past as simply as possible, both in respect to sets and costuming. The few furnishings are shared between the two eras, and transitions between them should involve little more than light and sound cues, and the quick draping of a few small pieces. It's remarkable what you can achieve through suggestion. Once the initial transition to the past has been achieved, the contemporary scenes may be played out without needing to reverse the process.

There is only one actor, Simon Lexner, who must inhabit both the present and past. Where the script indicates, he should fade away from the 21st century interludes while Max is still talking, and change quickly back into his 18th century clothes. Well organized crew and stage management should thoroughly rehearse his rapid changes with him. (Our stage manager was so efficient, she managed to play Heather Grenado while attending to the rest of the company.)

The watercolor butterfly painting is a key prop that is easy to lose track of. Be sure that it remains in the past during the present-day interludes, but returns in time to be gifted to Heather. For that matter, all of the props which are to go backward or forward must be tracked. Everyone should understand the two timelines and know when something is out of place.

The cabinet remains upstage throughout the play and is seen in both timelines throughout. Our cabinet was gimmicked with removable panels in the back, so that items could be removed or mysteriously appear inside. A black pipe and drape allowed crew to access the back of the cabinet unseen, though accessing this behind-the-cabinet area had to be accomplished during blackouts or transitional lighting cues. I had an authentically very old and ornate cabinet which I intended to use, but while trying to move it from my home, it fell apart, breaking irreparably before it reached my SUV. Instead, I had to take an inexpensive kitchen cabinet from Wal-Mart, but we painted and prettied it up well enough that it actually looked like an 18th century antique, from the back rows at least. Inexpensive, and it served its purpose.

I purchased two portable kitchen islands from IKEA, which were draped, and which had handy drawers near the top, and storage room at the base. The draping appeared only after the main time transition. Before that, they held crates of record albums, which disappeared nicely behind the draping, and stored a lot of props between shows.

We also used a kitchen cart, which rolled fairly easily around the stage. It was my wish that when Max would play records onstage, the audience would actually hear the vinyl playing live. For this purpose, I used a relatively inexpensive turntable that had a built-in blue-tooth transmitter. On the lower base, we had a portable car battery charger with an AC plug-in feature. Blue-tooth speakers were placed onstage. The battery unit was charged before every show, the turntable was plugged in and enabled, and the music played through the speakers nicely, while the cart could be freely moved about while trailing no cords. This method was not without its hazards.

Wherever possible, 33 rpm records and 45s were played on stage, but naturally, many sound cues had to be activated from the tech board; time transition sounds, atmospheric ambiance, and music when not emanating from a turntable. We had numerous music cues. Some of these were played onstage, a few had to be faked from the booth, and the final cue, Komm Susser Tod, was a hybrid, with live vocals superseding what we had pre-recorded. Productions could just as easily run every audio cue from the booth, as the transmitted blue-tooth audio got digitized in the process anyhow. Simplicity is your friend.

(I love the idea of playing real vinyl with the best possible fidelity. If you've got the gear and expertise, I wish you well.)

Bach's work is all in the public domain, but specific recordings are not. It is possible to find public domain recordings, but these are often from vintage 78 rpm sources, and sound tinny and crackly. Not the transporting glory that the story requires. There is no Irina Dobos, but there really is a Johanna Martzy, and her mid-century RCA recording of the Partitas were indeed re-pressed in about 2010 in an edition of only 250. There are less pricey releases, and it is easily purchased digitally, but you won't have the rights to use it in a dramatic context. I have been in the process of creating a virtually generated version, using midi files and very sophisticated, articulated virtual violin voices. Portions of this were tested in rehearsals, and it is reasonably convincing. For updates, see the Analog resources page at www.odsmil.com. (Schools and universities with adjacent drama and music departments could choose to record their own versions and showcase their students accordingly.)

*Historical and Genre Notes:* ANALOG came about as two early ideas were taking hold on my mind at the same time. The first: What if a particular vinyl record could elicit intense emotional responses and inexplicable events if listened to in the place it was recorded, and the second; What if someone secretly found a way to go back in time, and got impossible recordings of great composers performing or conducting their own works? I settled on J.S. Bach pretty early on, and chose the Chaconne after learning about the Johanna Martzy solo violin recording of the 1950s. Her performance of the Chaconne spurred me to conjure up the entirely fictitious Irena Dobos. By the way, that's pronounced DŌ-bōsh, with two long O's and a soft S.

I wound up reading up on the life of Bach pretty extensively, especially his letters, which gave me plenty of first-hand accounts of his day to day life. When he tells stories of scuffling with Geyersbach over a bad performance of his music, or complains of his inadequate salary, rails on about how Silbermann ought to well-temper the St. Thomas Church organ, or praises his student Altnickol, these details are all taken from his letters, or responses to them. I regret that one juicy anecdote, about how young Johann made love to his second cousin Maria Barbara, soon to become his wife, in the organ loft of

Blasius Church in Mühlhausen didn't fit anywhere. Bach didn't lead an especially dramatic life. He worked very hard, produced an astonishing canon, and lived as a dutiful man, earthy and fecund, but also deeply devout and disciplined in his calling. I suspect there could be a good one-man show that allows him to tell more of his story, but I could only provide a quick sketch.

His first child, Catherina Dorothea, was born in 1708, and I took advantage of the scarcity of biographical information about her to invent a backstory for her. We can infer that she faced hardship. We know she had to endure the loss of her mother and the early deaths of many of her younger siblings. (The more troubling aspects of her past in the script are fabrication) I took the liberty of rendering her name Katarina, which simply felt right to the ear. As the story developed, and Simon's violent and jealous past became clear, the idea of him engaging in a taboo tryst with Bach's daughter was hard to resist. It helped to prompt changes in both Max and his younger self as the story was lived or related.

The use of a vinyl record as a means of achieving time travel is patently absurd, but it was fun to try making it feel plausible, if only for a spell. Some attending early readings or the premiere production of the play thought after Act One that the story would launch into complicated paradoxes and multiple dimensions. (One apparently thought Max would reveal that he was Dr. Who) I had no intention of presenting this as a science fiction story. I simply needed a means to put Simon in the mid-18th century as a 'fish out of water,' and allow exactly the consequences that ensued. This isn't any kind of speculative fiction. It's a fantasy. There is some ambiguity at the end, and that's as it should be. There are questions that can't be answered. There will be no sequels. Audiences are free to interpret as they see fit.

By the way, it may have occurred to you that this story could have been sold as *Bach To The Future*. Numerous people involved with my production as well as assorted friends and colleagues came up with the same joke spontaneously. No doubt, other productions will as well.

*On Dialects:* The characters in the 18th century are understood to be native German speakers. However, I would strongly urge that they say their lines in their own natural voices, without affected dialect. By way of example, when you watch the movies of Amadeus or The Sound of Music, all of the characters are supposed to be speaking German, but they have a variety of British, American, and other accents. It is more natural to hear people speak and emote without affecting an accent. Of course, if the performer has a natural dialect, that will be the most natural and comfortable for the actor to use, and the audience to hear. We had an Uli Falkenrath from Puerto Rico who had a lovely, lilting Spanish diction that was all his own. It played as natural because it was.

This play has the potential to get over-complicated in its execution. Anywhere you can, simplify your staging, the better to emphasize the emotions and ideas behind the text. (In table readings, the story comes through well with no trappings other than music, just talented people inhabiting the roles and committing to the spell.) The science fiction elements are there to permit this specific tale to be told, but it is the human elements of obsession, love, regret and redemption which will stay with people. And don't forget to have fun!

Darryl Pickett,

January 2023

# About the Author

Darryl Pickett is an author, playwright, songwriter, actor, and former Walt Disney Imagineer. A native of New Mexico, he set out for Orlando in 1989, but returned to Albuquerque in 202, after over 32 years in the theme park/ themed entertainment industry. His debut novel, The Secret Feast of Father Christmas, appeared in 2011, and the suspense thriller Shark City Harbor grabbed readers in 2018. He has written numerous plays and musical theater pieces, including Trollop: the Trials and Tittilations of the INfamous Moll Flanders, which premiered in 2023. His next novel, The Magic Hour, will be his first set in his native Albuquerque.